MI
AND I

According to Swami Vivekananda

Compiled and Edited by
Swami Chetanananda

Foreword by
Christopher Isherwood

Advaita Ashrama
(PUBLICATION DEPARTMENT)
5 DEHI ENTALLY ROAD • KOLKATA 700 014

Published by
Swami Tattwavidananda
Adhyaksha, Advaita Ashrama
Mayavati, Champawat, Uttarakhand, Himalayas
from its Publication Department, Kolkata
Email: mail@advaitaashrama.org
Website: www.advaitaashrama.org

First American Edition, Published by
Vedanta Press, Hollywood in 1976

First Indian Edition, February 1980
Thirty-fourth Reprint, February 2015
6M6C

ISBN 978-81-85301-37-2

Printed in India at
Trio Process
Kolkata 700 014

CONTENTS

Publisher's Note	5
Foreword by Christopher Isherwood ...	7
Editor's Preface	17
Glimpses of Swami Vivekananda ...	21
Meditation According to Yoga ...	37
Meditation According to Vedanta ...	89

COVER DESIGN

'The light of a lamp does not flicker in a windless place': that is the simile which describes a yogi of one-pointed mind, who meditates upon the Atman.

*

There in the ignorant heart where
I dwell, by the grace of my mercy,
I am knowledge, that brilliant lamp,
dispelling its darkness.

(*Bhagavad-Gita*, VI. 19, X. 11)

PUBLISHER'S NOTE

It is being increasingly realized and recognized by modern psychologists that meditation should form part and parcel of the daily routine of everyone, in order to provide a counter-balance to the intensely active life that everyone is involved in the present-day world. Meditation calms the mind, brings self-composure, and enables one to concentrate one's mental powers. This is a great blessing on humanity that such a life is possible.

Swami Vivekananda has been acclaimed as a *dhyana-siddha*, one perfected in meditation, by Sri Ramakrishna himself, who had personally tried out with incredible rigorousness the diverse modes of meditation laid down in different paths and faiths. The Swami's *Raja-Yoga* is an authentic and a popular treatise on this subject. In his *Complete Works* (in 8 volumes), this subject is touched upon on several occasions.

Swami Chetanananda, Swami-in-Charge of the Vedanta Society, St. Louis (Missouri),

U.S.A., and formerly intimately associated with the publication work of our Ashrama, has carefully and painstakingly compiled Swami Vivekananda's thoughts on meditation and arranged them under suitable topical heads.

This book was first published in 1976 by the Vedanta Society of Southern California, Hollywood, U.S.A. The first Indian edition of it is now being published by us, for which the permission has been accorded by the Vedanta Society of Southern California. We are grateful to them.

In his Foreword to the book, Christopher Isherwood writes: 'What Swami Chetanananda has done here is to bring Vivekananda in person, as it were, to teach us how to meditate.' Further, he adds: 'Reading *his* (Swami Vivekananda's) printed words, we can catch something of the tone of his voice and even feel some sense of contact with his power.'

It is our privilege to provide this 'tone of his voice' and this 'contact with his power' to the readers by bringing out this Indian edition of the book.

18 February 1980
Advaita Ashrama, Mayavati

FOREWORD

'If only we had known him!' we say. Most of us take it for granted that we should be able to recognize a great spiritual teacher if we could meet one. Should we? Probably we flatter ourselves. ... Still, it must be agreed that a live teacher is vastly preferable to his dead book. Mere printed words can't usually convey the tone of their speaker's voice, much less the spiritual power behind that tone.

But Vivekananda is one of the rare exceptions. Reading *his* printed words, we can catch something of the tone of his voice and even feel some sense of contact with his power. Why is this?

Perhaps because most of these teachings were originally spoken, not written down, by him. They have the informality and urgency of speech. Furthermore, Vivekananda is speaking a language which we can understand but which is nevertheless inimitably his own, Vivekananda-English – that marvelously forceful idiom of quaintly-turned phrases and explosive exclamations. It recreates his personality for us even now, three-quarters of a century later.

What Swami Chetanananda has done here is to bring Vivekananda in person, as it were, to teach us how to meditate. These short self-contained extracts from his collected works tell us what religion is, why it is of vital concern to us and how we must practise it to make it part of our lives. Don't be in a hurry to read this book through to the end. Take one extract and think about it all day, or all week. Such instruction requires few words but demands unlimited after-thought.

Vivekananda's directness is disconcerting. He points his finger straight at you – like Uncle Sam in the old recruiting-posters. There can be no pretending to yourself that he is talking to somebody else. He means *you* and you had better listen.

You had better listen, says Vivekananda, because you do not know who you are. You imagine that you are Mr. or Ms. Jones. That is your fundamental, fatal mistake. Your opinion of yourself, be it high or low, is also mistaken; but that is of secondary importance. You may strut through life as the Emperor Jones or crawl through it as Jones the slave; it makes no difference. The Emperor Jones, if there were such a creature, would have subjects; the slave Jones would have a master. You have neither. For you are Brahman, eternal God, and, wherever you look, you see nothing but Brahman, wearing the many million disguises which are called by names as absurd as your own—Jones, Juarez, Jinnah, Jung, Jocho, Janvier, Jagatai, Jablochov; names which all mean the same thing, *I am not you*.

You do not know who you are because you are living in ignorance. This ignorance may seem pleasurable at moments but essentially it is a state of bondage and therefore misery. Your misery arises from the fact that Jones, as Jones, has got to die—while Brahman is eternal; and that Jones, as Jones, is other than Juarez, Jinnah and all the rest of them—while Brahman within all of them is one. Jones, in his illusion of separateness, is tormented by feelings of envy, hate, or fear toward these seemingly separate beings around him. Or else he feels drawn to some of them by desire or love and is tormented because he cannot possess them and become one with them completely.

Separateness, says Vivekananda, is an illusion which can and must be dispelled through love of the eternal Brahman within ourselves and within all our beings. Therefore the practice of religion is a denial of separateness and a renunciation of its objectives: fame, wealth, power over others.

I – Mr. or Ms. Jones – am made uneasy by these statements. I work for my possessions and I don't want to give them up. I am proud to be Jones and would hate to be Jablochov; besides, I suspect him of planning to take my possessions away from me. And then I am not just any old Jones, I am *the* Jones, the famous one, so I am unwilling to think of myself as an all-pervading non-person. I thoroughly approve of the word 'love'. But, to me, 'love' means Jane or John, and she or he is the most precious of all my possessions, whom I can only think of in exclusive relation to myself.

On the other hand, prudence advises me not to reject Vivekananda's teaching. My very uneasiness is an admission that what he says is at least partly true. I do get tense and depressed when I think about the future. My doctor has prescribed tranquilizers but they don't make me tranquil, only dull and sleepy. So why not devote a few minutes a day to this meditation? It's a kind of insurance, really. I take out hospital-insurance in the superstitious hope that it will save me from ever having to go into hospital. Why not take out Vivekananda-insurance in the hope that it will somehow save Jones from dying and losing his identity?

Good, says Vivekananda, with an indulgent smile. By all means make a start – even if it's for the wrong reason. He is endlessly good-humoured and patient. He never despairs of us because he knows – knows with the utter certainty of direct experience – that Brahman, our real nature, will gradually draw us to itself.

> So never mind these failures, these little backslidings. Hold the ideal a thousand times, and if you fail a thousand times, make the attempt once more. ... There is infinite life before the soul. Take your time and you will achieve your end.

This sounds almost too reassuring, too soothing. Can he be making fun of us? No and Yes. He means exactly what he says, but he is speaking in terms of the doctrine of reincarnation. When he says that we may take our time, he means that we are at liberty to remain in the bondage of ignorance for another thousand lifetimes; to go on dying and being reborn over and over again, until we have had enough of our separateness and have become seriously determined to end it. If we find Vivekananda's words reassuring – well, the joke is on us.

But what about *this* lifetime? Vivekananda once remarked:

> In trying to practice religion, eighty per cent of people turn cheats and about fifteen per cent go mad; only the remaining five per cent attain the immediate knowledge of the infinite Truth.

Does this shock you? If it does, imagine how you would react if you were told by the instructor at a gymnasium that, 'in trying to practise these exercises, eighty percent of my pupils cheat—by not doing the difficult exercises properly—and about fifteen percent over-exercise like madmen until they injure themselves and have to quit; only the remaining five percent really transform their physique.' Would you be surprised? Surely not, though you might well become depressed. You might decide, recognizing your own weakness, not to enrol at the gymnasium at all.

But there is no more miserable excuse for inaction than our claim to be weak, unspiritual, unworthy. When we make it, Vivekananda thunders at us that we are lions, not sheep; Brahman, not Jones. Then he turns gentle again and coaxes us to do something at least, to make some little effort, even if we are old, sick, burdened with dependents and worldly duties, hopelessly poor or hopelessly rich. He reminds us that true renunciation is mental, not necessarily physical. We are not required to disown our husbands or wives and turn our children out of doors. We must only try to realize that they are not really ours; to love them as dwelling-places of Brahman, not as mere individuals. We must realize also that our so-called possessions are just toys which have been lent to us to play with for a little while. A string of beads can be pretty. So can a diamond necklace. There is no danger in wearing the necklace when we have stopped being aware of their difference in price.

Again and again, Vivekananda makes us laugh, as he begs us not to waste time repenting, not to moan and groan over our sins: bids us dry our tears and see the fun in this mock-world which we have been taking so seriously. Thus, for a short while at least, he fills us with courage.

But Vivekananda did not devote all his tremendous energy to prodding forward the fainthearted ninety-five percent. He needed helpers in his work—dedicated men and women on whom he could rely—and for these he did not search among the weak. From time to time, unexpectedly, in the middle of a lecture, he would make one of his thrilling, resounding appeals to the strong, the still uncorrupted five per cent:

> Men and women of today! if there be among you any pure, fresh flower, let it be laid on the altar of God. If there are among you any who, being young, do not desire to return into the world, let them give up! Let them renounce! This is the one secret of spirituality, renunciation. Dare to do this. Be brave enough to do it. Such great sacrifices are necessary.
>
> Can you not see the tide of death and materialism that is rolling over these Western lands? Can you not see the power of lust and unholiness, that is eating into the very vitals of society? Believe me, you will not arrest these things by talk, or by movements of agitation for reform; but by renunciation, by standing up, in the midst of decay and death, as mountains of righteousness. Talk not, but let the power of purity, the power of chastity, the power of renunciation, emanate from every pore of your body. Let it strike those who are struggling day and

night for gold, that even in the midst of such a state of things, there can be one to whom wealth counts for nothing. Put away lust and wealth. Sacrifice yourselves.

But who is it that will do this? Not the worn-out or the old, bruised and battered by society, but the Earth's freshest and best, the strong, the young, the beautiful. Lay down your lives. Make yourselves servants of humanity. Be living sermons. This, and not talk, is renunciation.

Do not criticize others, for all doctrines and all dogmas are good; but show them by your lives that religion is no matter of books and beliefs, but of spiritual realization. Only those who have seen it will understand this; but such spirituality can be given to others, even though they be unconscious of the gift. Only those who have attained to this power are amongst the great teachers of mankind. They are the powers of light.

The more of such men any country produces, the higher is that country raised. That land where no such men

> exist, is doomed. Nothing can save it. Therefore my Master's message to the world is, 'Be ye all spiritual! Get ye first realization!'
>
> You have talked of the love of man, till the thing is in danger of becoming words alone. The time has come to act. The call now is, Do! Leap into the breach, and save the world!

Once, in my own life, I have heard that challenge echoed, in the simplest possible way. A group had gathered to discuss religious matters. Several of those present spoke at length and with eloquence about God and the life of prayer. Then, when the last of them had finished, a fourteen year-old boy exclaimed abruptly, with intense excitement: 'But—if that's all true—why do we ever do anything else?'

The question left us silent.

July 1974 Christopher Isherwood

EDITOR'S PREFACE

A fish, when caught in the fisherman's net and carried to the shore, flops and flounders on the dry land; struggles desperately to return to the water which is its real abode. Similarly, man's real home is God; he feels restless and disconsolate as long as he forgets his real nature, which is divine. Meditation is the bridge which connects man with God. The methods of meditation are many, but their main purpose is to provide a way to escape from the net of *maya* [Cosmic Illusion], the cause of all suffering, and to bring peace and bliss in the mind of man.

Buffeted by the tensions and anxieties, temptations and frustrations of the world around him, and at the same time finding only a great emptiness within himself, man today is in the midst of a crisis. He is unable to determine what are the lasting values of life. What he really seeks – perhaps without knowing it – is freedom, joy, poise and peace within. How can he achieve that? *Meditation is the answer.*

Specific instructions in the practice of meditation cannot be gathered from any book; rather, they must be learned from a qualified teacher and taught according to the temperament and spiritual advancement of the disciple. Nevertheless, the words of a great soul have a lasting power, and from these words of Swami Vivekananda one can not only become familiar with the general principles of meditation, but also gather inspiration and strength to seek the divinity that is within oneself. In reading these selections from Swami Vivekananda's lectures, writings, and conversations, it becomes evident that he taught with authority and not merely as a scholar. For he himself had plunged into the depths of the realization which he preached.

The book has been divided into two sections: 'Meditation according to Yoga' and 'Meditation according to Vedanta'. The first reflects the practical and mystical approach to meditation. The second is the more philosophical and transcendental approach. Both paths, however, emphasize meditation as the supreme means for attaining illumination and both direct the aspirant toward the same goal.

We have supplied a title for each selection, and definitions for some less familiar Sanskrit terms have been given within brackets in the body of the text. Also, for the sake of clarity and readability, we have occasionally cut one or more sentences or introductory phrases and modernized the punctuation without indicating these deletions or variations from the original. However, a reference to the volume and page number of the *Complete Works of Swami Vivekananda* is given for each selection, and a reference for each volume and its edition can be found on the last page of the book. Lastly, in choosing these excerpts, we have included not only Swami Vivekananda's instructions on meditation, but also some descriptions of his own experiences together with ancient stories he told and several of his recorded conversations, in order to try to reflect the rich variety of his teachings.

We are indebted to Advaita Ashrama, Mayavati, Himalayas, for giving us permission to reproduce these selections from the *Complete Works of Swami Vivekananda*. In conclusion, we would like to express our gratitude to Christopher Isherwood for writing the Foreword.

GLIMPSES OF SWAMI VIVEKANANDA

'Do you see a light when you are falling asleep?'

'Yes, I do. Doesn't everyone?' The boy's voice was filled with wonder.

It was soon after they had first met that Sri Ramakrishna asked Narendra this question and his reply provided the Master with a deep insight into the past, the nature, and the destiny of this remarkable youngster who would later become Swami Vivekananda. In his later years he himself described this supernormal faculty: 'From the earliest times that I can remember, I used to see a marvelous point of light between my eyebrows as soon as I shut my eyes to go to sleep, and I used to watch its various changes with great attention. That marvelous point of light would change colours and get bigger until it took the form of a ball; finally it would burst and cover my body from head to foot with white liquid light. As soon as that happened, I would lose outer consciousness and fall asleep. I used to believe that that was the way everybody went to sleep. Then, when I grew older and began to practise meditation, that point of light would appear to me as soon as I closed my eyes, and I would concentrate upon that.'

Swami Vivekananda's life story is that of a phenomenon. He was an ideal *yogi* and monk, teacher and leader, mystic and ascetic, worker and philosopher. He was capable of the most exalted devotion, yet possessed of the highest knowledge. He was a dedicated humanist, a musician and orator par excellence, and an accomplished athlete. In Vivekananda one catches a glimpse of the perfect man. His guru, Sri Ramakrishna, said about him: 'Narendra is a great soul – perfect in meditation. He cuts the veils of maya to pieces with the sword of knowledge. Inscrutable maya can never bring him under her control.'

The true nature of his exceptional disciple was revealed to Sri Ramakrishna in a vision even before their first meeting. Vivekananda was an ancient sage immersed in deep *samadhi* [transcendental consciousness], immovable as a rock. Sri Ramakrishna, master of samadhi, awakened that divine being from meditation, giving, as it were, a mighty push to that rock and directing it to course its way across the world, radiating spirituality and destroying narrowness and ignorance wherever it went.

Sri Ramakrishna told his other disciples this much of the visions he had about Narendra: 'One day I found that my mind was soaring high in samadhi along a luminous path. As it ascended higher and higher, I found on both sides of the way ideal forms of gods and goddesses. The mind then reached the outer limits of that region, where a luminous barrier separated the sphere of relative existence from that of the Absolute. Crossing that barrier, the mind entered the transcendental realm, where no corporeal being was visible. But the next moment I saw seven venerable sages seated there in samadhi. It occured to me that these sages must have surpassed not only men but even the gods in knowledge and holiness, in renunciation and love. Lost in admiration, I was reflecting on their greatness, when I saw a portion of that undifferentiated luminous region condense into the form of a divine child. The child came to one of the sages, tenderly clasped his neck with his lovely arms, and, addressing him in a sweet voice, tried to drag his mind down from the state of samadhi. That magic touch roused the sage from his superconscious state, and he fixed his half-open eyes upon the wonderful child. In great joy the strange child spoke to him, "I am going down. You too must go with me." The sage remained mute, but his tender look expressed his assent. No sooner had I seen Narendra than I recognized him to be that sage.' Later Ramakrishna disclosed the fact that the divine child was none other than himself.

Vivekananda was born on January 12, 1863, in Calcutta. From the beginning he was a precocious boy of exceptional energy. Yet his innate tendency toward meditation showed itself even in his early life. For along with the ordinary childhood games, he would play at meditation.

Once Narendra was meditating with his friends when a cobra appeared. The other boys were frightened and, shouting a warning to him, ran away. But Narendra remained motionless, and the cobra, after lingering about for a while, crawled away. Later he told his parents: 'I knew nothing of the snake or anything else. I was feeling inexpressible joy.'

At the age of fifteen he experienced spiritual ecstasy. He was journeying with his family to Raipur in Central India, and part of the trip had to be made in a bullock cart. On that particular day the air was crisp and clear, the trees and creepers were covered with blossoms, and birds of brilliant plumage sang in the forest. The cart was moving through a narrow pass where the lofty peaks rising on the two sides almost touched each other. Narendra caught sight of a large bee-hive in the cleft of a giant cliff that must have been there a very long time. Suddenly his mind was filled with awe and reverence for the Divine Providence, and he lost outer consciousness. Perhaps this was the first time that his powerful imagination had helped him to ascend to the realm of the superconscious.

Once during his days as a student, Vivekananda had a vision of Buddha which he related: 'While at school one night I was meditating behind closed doors and had a fairly deep concentration of mind. How long I meditated in that way I cannot say. It was over and I still kept my seat, when from the southern wall of that room a luminous figure stepped out and stood in front of me. It was the figure of a *sannyasin* [monk], absolutely calm, with shaven head, and staff and *kamandalu* [water pot] in either hand. He gazed at me for some time, and seemed as if he would address me. I, too, gazed at him in speechless wonder. Suddenly a kind of fright seized me. I opened the door and hurried out of the room. Then it struck me that it was foolish of me to run away like that, perhaps he might say something to me. But I have never seen that figure since. I think it was the Lord Buddha whom I saw.'

At one of their first meetings Sri Ramakrishna gave Vivekananda the magic touch which banished duality from his mind and gave him a taste of transcendental consciousness. Generally, the guru helps his disciple to attain samadhi as the goal of life. But Swami Vivekananda's guru had much higher expectations of his disciple. Sri Ramakrishna actually scolded Vivekananda for wanting to remain immersed in samadhi for three or four days at a stretch, breaking it only for food. 'Shame on you! You are asking for such an insignificant thing. I thought that you would be like a big banyan tree, and that thousands of people would rest in your shade. But now I see that you are seeking your own liberation.' Thus rebuked, Vivekananda shed tears, realizing the greatness of Sri Ramakrishna's heart.

At the Cossipore garden house, Vivekananda did experience *nirvikalpa samadhi* – the supreme realization of Vedanta as well as of Yoga. One evening, while he was meditating with Gopal senior, a brother-disciple, he felt as if a light had been placed behind his head. This light became more and more intense, and then he passed beyond all relativity and was lost in the Absolute. When he regained a little consciousness of the world, he was aware only of his head, but not the rest of his body. He cried out : 'Gopalda, where is my body?' 'Here it is, Naren,' answered Gopal, trying to reassure him. But when that failed to convince him, Gopal was terrified and hastened to inform Sri Ramakrishna, who only said: 'Let him stay in that state for a while! He has teased me long enough for it.'

After a long time Vivekananda returned to normal consciousness. An ineffable peace and joy filled his heart and mind. He came to the Master, who told him: 'Now the Divine Mother has shown you all. But this realization of yours shall be locked up for the present, and the key will remain with me. When you have finished doing Mother's work, this treasure will again be yours.'

Another interesting episode of this period was told by Girish Chandra Ghosh, a householder disciple of Sri Ramakrishna. One day Vivekananda and Girish sat under a tree to meditate. There were mosquitoes without number which disturbed Girish so much that he became restless. On opening his eyes he was amazed to see that Vivekananda's body was covered as if with a dark blanket, so great was the number of mosquitoes on him. But he was quite unconscious of their presence and had no recollection of them when he returned to normal consciousness.

After the passing away of Sri Ramakrishna, Vivekananda travelled all over India as an itinerant monk. He wanted to find a secluded place where he could live alone, absorbed in the contemplation of God. At this time the words of Buddha were guiding him: 'Even as the lion, not trembling at noises; even as the wind, not caught in a net; even as the lotus-leaf, untouched by the water – so do thou wander alone like the rhinoceros !' But Divine Providence had other plans for him, and he could not escape his destiny. As he was to write later : 'Nothing in my whole life ever so filled me with the sense of work to be done. It was as if I were *thrown out* from that life in caves to wander to and fro in the plains below.'

One day during his travels in the Himalayas he sat to meditate under a pepul tree by the side of a stream. There he realized the oneness of the universe and man, that man is a universe in miniature. He realized that all that exists in the universe also exists in the body, and further, that the whole universe can be found contained in a single atom. He jotted down this experience in a notebook and told his brother-disciple and companion, Swami Akhandananda: 'Today I found the solution to one of life's most difficult problems. It was revealed to me that the macrocosm and the microcosm are guided by the same principle.'

On May 31, 1893, Vivekananda began his journey to Chicago to take part in the Parliament of Religions as a representative of Hinduism. But his message was so universal that one observer commented: 'Vivekananda was the representative of all religions of the world.' He proclaimed the supreme message of Vedanta: 'Ye are the children of God, the sharers of Immortal Bliss, holy and perfect beings. Ye divinities on earth – sinners ! It is a sin to call a man so; it is a standing libel on human nature !'

For the next three years he travelled extensively in the United States and in many European countries. Yet the active life of the West could not disturb his meditation. In Vivekananda we find the two opposing currents of action and meditation flowing harmoniously, never interfering with each other.

Being nearly exhausted by the uninterrupted work of public lecturing and classes, in the beginning of June 1895, the Swami accepted an invitation from Mr. Francis Leggett to go to Percy, New Hampshire, for a period of rest in the silence of the pine woods. Here also he experienced nirvikalpa samadhi. In a letter from Percy, dated June 7, 1895, he wrote to Mrs. Ole Bull:

'This is one of the most beautiful spots I have ever seen. Imagine a lake surrounded with hills covered with a huge forest, with nobody but ourselves. So lovely, so quiet, so restful and you may imagine how glad I am to be here after the bustle of the cities.

'It gives me a new lease on life to be here. I go into the forest alone and read my *Gita* and am quite happy. I will leave this place in about ten days and go to Thousand Island Park. I will meditate by the hour there and be all alone to myself. The very idea is ennobling.'

In Indian art and architecture, the state of realization, or supreme enlightenment, has been depicted in the meditating form of Buddha, the Enlightened One. This same lofty ideal can be seen in Swami Vivekananda in the memoir of Mrs. Mary Funke, who was one of his disciples :

'The last day [at Thousand Island Park] has been a very wonderful and precious one. He asked Christine and me to take a walk, as he wished to be alone with us. We went up a hill about half a mile away. All was woods and solitude. Finally he selected a low-branched tree, and we sat under the spreading branches. Instead of the expected talk, he suddenly said, "Now we will meditate. We shall be like Buddha under the Bo-tree." He seemed to turn to bronze, so still was he. Then a thunderstorm came up and it poured. He never noticed it. I raised my unbrella and protected him as much as possible. Completely absorbed in his meditation, he was oblivious of everything. Soon we heard shouts in the distance. The others had come out after us with raincoats and umbrellas. Swamiji looked around regretfully, for we *had* to go, and said, "Once more am I in Calcutta in the rains." '

One must not forget that Vivekananda, as Sri Ramakrishna had said, was not an ordinary man, but a *nitya-siddha*, one who is born perfect, an *Ishvarakoti* or special messenger of God born on earth to fulfil a divine mission. Vivekananda said: 'I shall inspire men everywhere, until the world shall know that it is one with God.'

All through his life he practised concentration so much that it became a part of him. In the West he had to control this precious habit. Sister Nivedita tells us : 'On one occasion, teaching a New York class to meditate, it was found at the end that he could not be brought back to consciousness, and one by one his students stole quietly away. But he was deeply mortified when he knew what had happened, and never risked its repetition. Meditating in private, with one or two, he would give a word by which he could be recalled.'

While staying at Camp Irving in Northern California, one morning the Swami found Shanti [Mrs Hansborough] in the kitchen preparing food when it was time for his morning class. 'Aren't you coming in to meditate?' he asked. Shanti replied that she had neglected to plan her work properly, so now she had to stay in the kitchen. Swamiji said: 'Well, never mind. Our master said you could leave meditation for service. All right. I will meditate for you.' Shanti said later : 'All through the class I felt he really was meditating for me.'

With the approaching end of his mission and earthly life Vivekananda realized ever more clearly how like a stage this world is. His eyes were now looking increasingly at the light of another world, his real abode. And how vividly and touchingly he expressed his yearning to return to it in his letter of April 18, 1900, written from California to Miss Josephine MacLeod, his ever loyal 'Joe':

'Work is always difficult. Pray for me, Joe, that my work may stop forever and my whole soul be absorbed in Mother. Her work She knows.

'I am well, very well mentally. I feel the rest of the soul more than that of the body. The battles are lost and won. I have bundled my things and am waiting for the Great Deliverer.

'Siva, O Siva, carry my boat to the other shore !

'After all, Joe, I am only the boy who used to listen with rapt wonderment to the wonderful words of Sri Ramakrishna under the banyan at Dakshineswar. That is my true nature – works and activities, doing good and so forth, are all superimpositions. Now I again hear his voice, the same old voice thrilling my soul. Bonds are breaking – love dying, work becoming tasteless – the glamour is off life. Now only the voice of the Master calling – "I come, Lord, I come" – "Let the dead bury the dead. Follow thou me."

'Yes, I come. Nirvana is before me. I feel it at times, the same infinite ocean of peace, without a ripple, a breath.

'Oh, it is so calm !'

Sri Ramakrishna had prophesied that Narendra would merge in nirvikalpa samadhi at the end of his work, when he realized who and what he really was. One day at the Belur Math when a brother-disciple asked him casually, 'Do you know yet who you are, Swamiji?' he was awed into silence by the unexpected reply, 'Yes, I know now.'

Vivekananda's exit from the world was as wonderful as his entry into it. After consulting an almanac, he chose an auspicious day to end his drama. It was the 4th of July, 1902. He meditated for three hours that morning and conducted a class on Sanskrit grammar and Vedanta philosophy for the young monks in the afternoon, after which he took a long walk with one of his brother-disciples.

Of his life's final moments, Sister Nivedita has left this account: 'On his return from this walk, the bell was ringing for even-song, and he went to his own room, and sat down facing towards the Ganges, to meditate. It was the last time. Then on the wings of that meditation, his spirit soared whence there could be no return, and the body was left, like a folded vesture, on the earth.'

Swami Vivekananda's last words, spoken to a monastic disciple who was attending him, were: 'Wait and meditate till I call you.'

Vedanta Society
of Southern California
Vivekananda's Birthday
January 14, 1974

S.C.

MEDITATION ACCORDING TO YOGA

Thinking about sense-objects
Will attach you to sense-objects;
Grow attached, and you become addicted;
Thwart your addiction, it turns to anger;
Be angry, and you confuse your mind;
Confuse your mind, you forget the lesson
of experience;
Forget experience, you lose discrimination;
Lose discrimination, and you miss life's
only purpose.

*

The uncontrolled mind
Does not guess that the Atman is present:
How can it meditate?
Without meditation, where is peace?
Without peace, where is happiness?

(*Bhagavad-Gita*, II. 62, 63, 65)

WHAT IS MEDITATION?

What is meditation? Meditation is the power which enables us to resist all this [our slavery to nature]. Nature may call us, 'Look, there is a beautiful thing!' I do not look. Now she says, 'There is a beautiful smell; smell it!' I say to my nose, 'Do not smell it,' and the nose doesn't. 'Eyes, do not see!' Nature does such an awful thing—kills one of my children, and says, 'Now, rascal, sit down and weep! Go to the depths!' I say, 'I don't have to.' I jump up. I must be free. Try it sometimes. In meditation, for a moment you can change this nature. Now, if you had that power in yourself, would not that be heaven, freedom? That is the power of meditation.

How is it to be attained? In a dozen different ways. Each temperament has its own way. But this is the general principle: get hold of the mind. The mind is like a lake, and every stone that drops into it raises waves. These waves do not let us see what we are. The full moon is reflected in the water of the lake, but the surface is so disturbed that we do not see the reflection clearly. Let it be calm. Do not let nature raise the wave. Keep quiet, and then after a little while she will give you up. Then we know what we are. God is there already, but the mind is so agitated, always running after the senses. You close the senses and yet you whirl and whirl about. Just this moment I think I am all right and I will meditate upon God, and then my mind goes to London in one minute. And if I pull it away from there, it goes to New York to think about the things I have done there in the past. These waves are to be stopped by the power of meditation. (IV. 248)

THE GATE TO BLISS

Meditation is the gate that opens that [infinite joy] to us. Prayers, ceremonials and all the other forms of worship are simply kindergartens of meditation. You pray, you offer something. A certain theory existed that everything raised one's spiritual power. The use of certain words, flowers, images, temples, ceremonials like the waving of lights brings the mind to that attitude, but that attitude is always in the human soul, nowhere else. People are all doing it; but what they do without knowing it, do knowingly. That is the power of meditation.

Slowly and gradually we are to train ourselves. It is no joke—not a question of a day, or years, or maybe of births. Never mind! The pull must go on. Knowingly, voluntarily, the pull must go on. Inch by inch we will gain ground. We will begin to feel and get real possessions, which no one can take away from us—the wealth that no man can take, the wealth that nobody can destroy, the joy that no misery can hurt any more. (IV. 249, 248)

IN SEARCH OF TRUTH

Yoga is the science which teaches us how to get these perceptions [direct experiences of God]. It is not much use to talk about religion until one has felt it. Why is there so much disturbance, so much fighting and quarrelling in the name of God? There has been more bloodshed in the name of God than for any other cause, because people never went to the fountain-head; they were content only to give a mental assent to the customs of their forefathers, and wanted others to do the same. What right has a man to say he has a soul if he does not feel it, or that there is a God if he does not see Him? If there is a God we must see Him, if there is a soul we must perceive it; otherwise it is better not to believe. It is better to be an outspoken atheist than a hypocrite.

Man wants truth, wants to experience truth for himself; when he has grasped it, realized it, felt it within his heart of hearts, then alone, declare the Vedas, would all doubts vanish, all darkness be scattered and all crookedness be made straight. (I. 127-28)

HOW RESTLESS IS THE MIND!

How hard it is to control the mind!. Well has it been compared to the maddened monkey. There was a monkey, restless by his own nature, as all monkeys are. As if that were not enough someone made him drink freely of wine, so that he became still more restless. Then a scorpion stung him. When a man is stung by a scorpion, he jumps about for a whole day; so the poor monkey found his condition worse than ever. To complete his misery a demon entered into him. What language can describe the uncontrollable restlessness of that monkey? The human mind is like that monkey, incessantly active by its own nature; then it becomes drunk with the wine of desire, thus increasing its turbulence. After desire takes possession comes the sting of the scorpion of jealousy at the success of others, and last of all the demon of pride enters the mind, making it think itself of all importance. How hard to control such a mind! (I. 174)

A TREMENDOUS TASK

According to the Yogis, there are three principal nerve currents: one they call the Ida, the other the Pingala, and the middle one the Sushumna, and all these are inside the spinal column. The Ida and the Pingala, the left and the right, are clusters of nerves, while the middle one, the Sushumna, is hollow and is not a cluster of nerves. This Sushumna is closed, and for the ordinary man is of no use, for he works through the Ida and the Pingala only. Currents are continually going down and coming up through these nerves, carrying orders all over the body through other nerves running to the different organs of the body.

The task before us is vast; and first and foremost, we must seek to control the vast mass of sunken thoughts which have become automatic with us. The evil deed is, no doubt, on the conscious plane; but the cause which produced the evil deed was far beyond in the realms of the unconscious, unseen, and therefore more potent.

This is the first part of the study, the control of the unconscious. The next is to go beyond the conscious [the waking state]. So, therefore, we see now that there must be a twofold work. First, by the proper working of the Ida and the Pingala, which are the two existing ordinary currents, to control the subconscious action; and secondly, to go beyond even [the surface] consciousness.

He alone is the Yogi who, after long practice in self-concentration, has attained to this truth. The Sushumna now opens and a current which never before entered into this new passage will find its way into it, and gradually ascend to (what we call in figurative language) the different lotus centres, till at last it reaches the brain. Then the Yogi becomes conscious of what he really is, God himself. (II. 30, 34-36)

ENVIRONMENT FOR MEDITATION

Those of you who can afford it will do better to have a room for this practice alone. Do not sleep in that room, it must be kept holy. You must not enter the room until you have bathed, and are perfectly clean in body and mind. Place flowers in that room always; they are the best surroundings for a Yogi; also pictures that are pleasing. Burn incense morning and evening. Have no quarrelling, nor anger, nor unholy thought in that room. Only allow those persons to enter it who are of the same thought as you. Then gradually there will be an atmosphere of holiness in the room, so that when you are miserable, sorrowful, doubtful, or your mind is disturbed, the very fact of entering that room will make you calm. This was the idea of the temple and the church, and in some temples and churches you will find it even now, but in the majority of them the very idea has been lost. The idea is that by keeping holy vibrations there the place becomes and remains illumined. Those who cannot afford to have a room set apart can practise anywhere they like. (I. 145)

REQUISITES FOR MEDITATION

Where there is fire, or in water or on ground which is strewn with dry leaves, where there are many ant-hills, where there are wild animals, or danger, where four streets meet, where there is too much noise, where there are many wicked persons, Yoga must not be practised. This applies more particularly to India.

Do not practise when the body feels very lazy or ill, or when the mind is very miserable and sorrowful. Go to a place which is well hidden, and where people do not come to disturb you. Do not choose dirty places. Rather choose beautiful scenery, or a room in your own house which is beautiful. When you practise, first salute all the ancient Yogis, and your own Guru, and God, and then begin. (I. 192)

TIME FOR MEDITATION

You must practise at least twice every day, and the best times are towards the morning and the evening. When night passes into day, and day into night, a state of relative calmness ensues. The early morning and the early evening are the two periods of calmness. Your body will have a like tendency to become calm at those times. We should take advantage of that natural condition and begin then to practise. Make it a rule not to eat until you have practised; if you do this, the sheer force of hunger will break your laziness. In India they teach children never to eat until they have practised or worshipped, and it becomes natural to them after a time; a boy will not feel hungry until he has bathed and practised. (I. 144-45)

NOW PRAY!

Mentally repeat:

Let all beings be happy;
Let all beings be peaceful;
Let all beings be blissful.

So do to the east, south, north and west. The more you do that the better you will feel yourself. You will find at last that the easiest way to make ourselves healthy is to see that others are healthy, and the easiest way to make ourselves happy is to see that others are happy. After doing that, those who believe in God should pray—not for money, not for health, nor for heaven; pray for knowledge and light; every other prayer is selfish. (I. 145-46)

THE FIRST LESSON

Sit for some time and let the mind run on. You simply wait and watch. Knowledge is power, says the proverb, and that is true. Until you know what the mind is doing you cannot control it. Give it the rein; many hideous thoughts may come into it; you will be astonished that it was possible for you to think such thoughts. But you will find that each day the mind's vagaries are becoming less and less violent, that each day it is becoming calmer.

Give up all argumentation and other distractions. Is there anything in dry intellectual jargon? It only throws the mind off its balance and disturbs it. Things of subtler planes have to be realized. Will talking do that? So give up all vain talk. Read only those books which have been written by persons who have had realization. (I. 174, 176-77)

NOW THINK!

Think of your own body, and see that it is strong and healthy; it is the best instrument you have. Think of it as being as strong as adamant, and that with the help of this body you will cross the ocean of life. Freedom is never to be reached by the weak. Throw away all weakness. Tell your body that it is strong, tell your mind that it is strong, and have unbounded faith and hope in yourself. (I. 146)

A FEW EXAMPLES OF MEDITATION

Imagine a lotus upon the top of the head, several inches up, with virtue as its centre, and knowledge as its stalk. The eight petals of the lotus are the eight powers of the Yogi. Inside, the stamens and pistils are renunciation. If the Yogi refuses the external powers he will come to salvation. So the eight petals of the lotus are the eight powers, but the internal stamens and pistils are extreme renunciation, the renunciation of all these powers. Inside of that lotus think of the Golden One, the Almighty, the Intangible, He whose name is Om, the Inexpressible, surrounded with effulgent light. Meditate on that.

Another meditation is given: Think of a space in your heart, and in the midst of that space think that a flame is burning. Think of that flame as your own soul and inside the flame is another effulgent light, and that is the Soul of your soul, God. Meditate upon that in the heart. (I. 192-93)

HOW TO REACH THE GOAL

Practise hard; whether you live or die does not matter. You have to plunge in and work, without thinking of the result. If you are brave enough, in six months you will be a perfect Yogi. But those who take up just a bit of it and a little of everything else make no progress. It is of no use simply to take a course of lessons.

To succeed, you must have tremendous perseverance, tremendous will. 'I will drink the ocean,' says the persevering soul, 'at my will mountains will crumble up.' Have that sort of energy, that sort of will, work hard, and you will reach the goal. (I. 178)

BE CAREFUL!

Every motion is in a circle. If you can take up a stone, and project it into space, and then live long enough, that stone, if it meets with no obstruction, will come back exactly to your hand. Just as in the case of electricity the modern theory is that the power leaves the dynamo and completes the circle back to the dynamo, so with hate and love; they must come back to the source. Therefore do not hate anybody, because that hatred which comes out from you, must, in the long run, come back to you. If you love, that love will come back to you, completing the circle. (I. 196)

THE MIND-LAKE

The bottom of a lake we cannot see, because its surface is covered with ripples. It is only possible for us to catch a glimpse of the bottom, when the ripples have subsided, and the water is calm. If the water is muddy or is agitated all the time, the bottom will not be seen. If it is clear, and there are no waves, we shall see the bottom. The bottom of the lake is our own true Self; the lake is the Chitta [mind-stuff] and the waves the Vrittis [thought-waves].

Again, the mind is in three states, one of which is darkness, called Tamas, found in brutes and idiots; it only acts to injure. No other idea comes into that state of mind. Then there is the active state of mind, Rajas, whose chief motives are power and enjoyment. 'I will be powerful and rule others.' Then there is the state called Sattva, serenity, calmness, in which the waves cease, and the water of the mind-lake becomes clear. (I. 202)

MIND AND ITS CONTROL

Meditation is one of the great means of controlling the rising of these [thought] waves. By meditation you can make the mind subdue these waves, and if you go on practising meditation for days, and months, and years until it has become a habit, until it will come in spite of yourself, anger and hatred will be controlled and checked. (I. 242-43)

BE CHEERFUL!

The first sign that you are becoming religious is that you are becoming cheerful. When a man is gloomy, that may be dyspepsia, but it is not religion.

To the Yogi, everything is bliss, every

human face that he sees brings cheerfulness to him. That is the sign of a virtuous man. What business have you with clouded faces? It is terrible. If you have a clouded face, do not go out that day, shut yourself up in your room. What right have you to carry this disease out into the world? (I. 264-65)

THE SIGNS OF A YOGI

'He who hates none, who is the friend of all, who is merciful to all, who has nothing of his own, who is free from egoism, who is even-minded in pain and pleasure, who is forbearing, who is always satisfied, who works always in Yoga, whose self has become controlled, whose will is firm, whose mind and intellect are given up unto Me, such a one is My beloved Bhakta [devotee]. From whom comes no disturbance, who cannot be disturbed by others, who is free from joy, anger, fear, and anxiety, such a one is My beloved. He who does not depend on anything, who is pure and active, who does not care whether good comes or evil, and never becomes miserable, who has given up all efforts for himself, who is the same in praise or in blame, with a silent, thoughtful mind, blessed with what little comes in his way, homeless, for the whole world is his home, and who is steady in his ideas, such a one is My beloved Bhakta.'

Such alone become Yogis. (I. 193)

BE LIKE A PEARL OYSTER

There is a pretty Indian fable to the effect that if it rains when the star Svati is in the ascendant, and a drop of rain falls into an oyster, that drop becomes a pearl. The oysters know this, so they come to the surface when that star shines, and wait to catch the precious raindrop. When a drop falls into them, quickly the oysters close their shells and dive down to the bottom of the sea, there to patiently develop the drop into the pearl. We should be like that. First hear, then understand, and then, leaving all distractions, shut your minds to outside influences, and devote yourselves to developing the truth within you. (I. 177)

PATIENCE

There was a great god-sage called Narada. Just as there are sages among mankind, great Yogis, so there are great Yogis among the gods. Narada was a good Yogi, and very great. He travelled everywhere. One day he was passing through a forest, and saw a man who had been meditating until the white ants had built a huge mound round his body—so long had he been sitting in that position. He said to Narada, 'Where are you going?' Narada replied, 'I am going to heaven.' 'Then ask God when He will be merciful to me; when I shall attain freedom.' Further on Narada saw another man. He was jumping about, singing, dancing, and said, 'O Narada, where are you going?' His voice and his gestures were wild. Narada said, 'I am going to heaven.' 'Then, ask when I shall be free.' Narada went on.

In the course of time he came again by the same road, and there was the man who had been meditating with the ant-hill round him. He said, 'O Narada, did you ask the Lord about me?' 'Oh, yes.' 'What did He say?' 'The Lord told me that you would attain freedom in four more births.' Then the man began to weep and wail, and said, 'I have meditated until an ant-hill has grown around me, and I have four more births yet !'

Narada went to the other man. 'Did you ask my question?' 'Oh, yes. Do you see this tamarind tree? I have to tell you that as many leaves as there are on that tree, so many times you shall be born, and then you shall attain freedom.' The man began to dance for joy, and said, 'I shall have freedom after such a short time !'

A voice came: 'My child, you will have freedom this minute.' That was the reward for his perseverance. He was ready to work through all those births, nothing discouraged him. (I. 193-94)

IN THE REALM OF TRANQUILLITY

The greatest help to spiritual life is meditation. In meditation we divest ourselves of all material conditions and feel our divine nature. We do not depend upon any external help in meditation. The touch of the soul can paint the brightest colour even in the dingiest places; it can cast a fragrance over the vilest thing; it can make the wicked divine – and all enmity, all selfishness is effaced. The less the thought of the body, the better. For it is the body that drags us down. It is attachment, identification, which makes us miserable. That is the secret: To think that I am the spirit and not the body, and that the whole of this universe with all its relations, with all its good and all its evil, is but a series of paintings – scenes on a canvas – of which I am the witness. (II. 37)

TRANSFORMATION THROUGH MEDITATION

There was a young man that could not in any way support his family. He was strong and vigorous and, finally, became a highway robber; he attacked persons in the street and robbed them, and with that money he supported his father, mother, wife and children. This went on continually, until one day a great saint called Narada was passing by, and the robber attacked him.

The sage asked the robber, 'Why are you going to rob me? It is a great sin to rob human beings and kill them. What do you incur all this sin for?' The robber said, 'Why, I want to support my family with this money.' 'Now,' said the sage, 'do you think that they take a share of your sin also?' 'Certainly they do,' replied the robber. 'Very good,' said the sage, 'make me safe by tying me up here, while you go home and ask your people whether they will share your sin in the same way as they share the money you make.'

The man accordingly went to his father, and asked, 'Father, do you know how I support you?' He answered, 'No, I do not.' 'I am a robber, and I kill persons and rob them.' 'What! you do that, my son? Get away! You outcast!' He then went to his mother and asked her, 'Mother, do you know how I support you?' 'No,' she replied. 'Through robbery and murder.' 'How horrible it is!' cried the mother. 'But, do you partake in my sin?' said the son. 'Why should I? I never committed a robbery,' answered the mother.

Then he went to his wife and questioned her, 'Do you know how I maintain you all?' 'No,' she responded. 'Why, I am a highway-man,' he rejoined, 'and for years have been robbing people; that is how I support and maintain you all. And what I now want to know is, whether you are ready to share in my sin.' 'By no means. You are my husband, and it is your duty to support me.'

The eyes of the robber were opened. 'That is the way of the world – even my nearest relatives, for whom I have been robbing, will not share in my destiny.' He came back to the place where he had bound the sage, unfastened his bonds, fell at his feet, recounted everything and said, 'Save me! What can I do?'

The sage said, 'Give up your present course of life. You see that none of your family really loves you, so give up all these delusions. They will share your prosperity; but the moment you have nothing they will desert you. There is none who will share in your evil, but they will all share in your good. Therefore, worship Him who alone stands by us whether we are doing good or evil. He never leaves us, for love never drags down, knows no barter, no selfishness.'

Then the sage taught him how to worship. And this man left everything and went into a forest. There he went on praying and meditating until he forgot himself so entirely that the ants came and built ant-hills around him, and he was quite unconscious of it.

After many years had passed, a voice came saying, 'Arise, O sage!' Thus aroused he exclaimed, 'Sage? I am a robber!' 'No more "robber",' answered the voice, 'a purified sage art thou. Thine old name is gone. But now, since thy meditation was so deep and great that thou didst not remark even the ant-hills which surrounded thee, henceforth, thy name shall be Valmiki[1] – "he that was born in the ant-hill".' So, he became a sage. (IV. 63-65)

THREE STAGES OF MEDITATION

There are three stages in meditation. The first is what is called Dharana, concentrating

---

1. Valmiki is the author of the great epic *Ramayana*.

the mind upon an object. I try to concentrate my mind upon this glass, excluding every other object from my mind except this glass. But the mind is wavering. When it has become strong and does not waver so much, it is called Dhyana, meditation. And then there is a still higher state when the differentiation between the glass and myself is lost—Samadhi or absorption. The mind and the glass are identical. I do not see any difference. All the senses stop and all powers that have been working through other channels of other senses are focused in the mind. Then this glass is under the power of the mind entirely. This is to be realized. It is a tremendous play played by the Yogis. (IV. 228)

HOW TO REST

Meditation means the mind is turned back upon itself. The mind stops all the thought-waves and the world stops. Your consciousness expands. Every time you meditate you will keep your growth. Work a little harder, more and more, and meditation comes. You do not feel the body or anything else. When you come out of it after the hour, you have had the most beautiful rest you ever had in your life. That is the only way you ever give rest to your system. Not even the deepest sleep will give you such rest as that. The mind goes on jumping even in deepest sleep. Just those few minutes in meditation your brain has almost stopped. Just a little vitality is kept up. You forget the body. You may be cut to pieces and not feel it at all. You feel such pleasure in it. You become so light. This is the perfect rest we will get in meditation. (IV. 235)

ACTION BRINGS REACTION

In every phenomenon in nature you contribute at least half and nature brings half. If your half is taken off, the thing must stop.

To every action there is equal reaction. If a man strikes me and wounds me, it is that man's action and my body's reaction.

Let us take another example. You are dropping stones upon the smooth surface of a lake. Every stone you drop is followed by a reaction. The stone is covered by the little waves in the lake. Similarly, external things are like the stones dropping into the lake of the mind. So we do not really see the external; we see the wave only. (IV. 228, 229)

THE POWER OF MEDITATION

The power of meditation gets us everything.

If you want to get power over nature, you can have it through meditation. It is through the power of meditation all scientific facts are discovered today. They study the subject and forget everything their own identity and everything, and then the great fact comes like a flash. Some people think that is inspiration.

There is no inspiration. Whatever passes for inspiration is the result that comes from causes already in the mind. One day, flash comes the result! Their past work was the cause.

Therein also you see the power of meditation – intensity of thought. These men churn up their own souls. Great truths come to the surface and become manifest. Therefore the practice of meditation is the great scientific method of knowledge. (IV. 230)

MEDITATION IS A SCIENCE

Whatever exists is one. There cannot be many. That is what is meant by science and knowledge. Ignorance sees manifold. Knowledge realizes one. Reducing the many into one is science. The whole of the universe has been demonstrated into one. That science is called the science of Vedanta. The whole universe is one.

We have all these variations now and we see them—what we call the five elements: solid, liquid, gaseous, luminous, ethereal. Meditation consists in this practice of dissolving everything into the ultimate Reality—spirit. The solid melts into liquid, that into gas, gas into ether, then mind, and mind will melt away. All is spirit.

Meditation, you know, comes by a process of imagination. You go through all these processes of purification of the elements—making the one melt into the other, that into the next higher, that into mind, that into spirit, and then you are spirit.

Here is a huge mass of clay. Out of that clay I made a little mouse and you made a little elephant. Both are clay. Melt both down. They are essentially one. (IV. 232-35)

PAVHARI BABA: AN IDEAL YOGI

Everyone has heard of the thief who had come to steal from his [Pavhari Baba's] Ashrama, and who at the sight of the saint got frightened and ran away, leaving the goods he had stolen in a bundle behind; how the saint took the bundle up, ran after the thief, and came up to him after miles of hard running; how the saint laid the bundle at the feet of the thief, and with folded hands and tears in his eyes asked his pardon for his own intrusion, and begged hard for his acceptance of the goods, since they belonged to him, and not to himself.

We are also told, on reliable authority, how once he was bitten by a cobra; and though he was given up for hours as dead, he revived; and when his friends asked him about it, he only replied that the cobra 'was a messenger from the Beloved'.

One of his great peculiarities was his entire absorption at the time in the task in hand, however trivial. The same amount of care and attention was bestowed in cleaning a copper pot as in the worship of Sri Raghunathji [Ramachandra, his chosen ideal of God] – he himself being the best example of the secret he once told us of work: 'The means should be loved and cared for as if it were the end itself.'

The present writer [Swami Vivekananda] had occasion to ask the saint the reason of his not coming out of his cave to help the world. He gave the following reply: 'Do you think that physical help is the only help possible? Is it not possible that one mind can help other minds even without the activity of the body?' (IV. 292-94)

A FABLE ABOUT BUDDHA

When Buddha was born, he was so pure that whosoever looked at his face from a distance immediately gave up the ceremonial religion and became a monk and became saved. So the gods held a meeting. They said, 'We are undone.' Because most of the gods live upon the ceremonials. These sacrifices go to the gods and these sacrifices were all gone. The gods were dying of hunger and the reason for it was that their power was gone.

So the gods said: 'We must, anyhow, put this man down. He is too pure for our life.' And then the gods came and said [to Buddha]: 'Sir, we come to ask you something. We want to make a great sacrifice and we mean to make a huge fire, and we have been seeking all over the world for a pure spot to light the fire on and could not find it, and now we have found it. If you will lie down, on your breast we will make the huge fire.' 'Granted,' he says, 'go on.'

And the gods built the fire high upon the breast of Buddha, and they thought he was dead, and he was not. And then they went about and said, 'We are undone.' And all the gods began to strike him. No good. They could not kill him. From underneath, the voice comes: 'Why are you making all these vain attempts?'

'Whoever looks upon you becomes purified and is saved, and nobody is going to worship us.'

'Then, your attempt is vain, because purity can never be killed.' (III. 525)

A SONG OF SAMADHI

(Rendered from Bengali)

Lo! The sun is not, nor the comely moon,
All light extinct; in the great void of space
Floats shadow-like the image-universe.

In the void of mind involute, there floats
The fleeting universe, rises and floats,
Sinks again, ceaseless, in the current 'I'.

Slowly, slowly, the shadow-multitude
Entered the primal womb, and flowed
ceaseless,
The only current, the 'I am', 'I am'.
Lo! 'Tis stopped, ev'n that current flows no
more,
Void merged into void – beyond speech
and mind!
Whose heart understands, he verily does.

(IV. 498)

QUESTIONS AND ANSWERS

Question: Whom can we call a Guru?

Swami Vivekananda: He who can tell your past and future is your Guru.

Q: How can one have Bhakti [devotion]?

Swamiji: There is Bhakti within you, only a veil of lust and wealth covers it, and as soon as that is removed Bhakti will manifest by itself.

Q: Does the Kundalini [spiritual energy] really exist in the physical body?

Swamiji: Sri Ramakrishna used to say that the so-called lotuses of the Yogi do not really exist in the human body, but that they are created within oneself by Yoga powers.

Q: Can a man attain Mukti [liberation] by image-worship?

Swamiji: Image-worship cannot directly give Mukti; it may be an indirect cause, a help on the way. Image-worship should not be condemned for, with many, it prepares the mind for the realization of the Advaita [non-duality] which alone makes man perfect.

Q: What is Mukti?

Swamiji: Mukti means entire freedom —freedom from the bondages of good and evil. A golden chain is as much a chain as an iron one. Sri Ramakrishna used to say that to pick out one thorn which has stuck into the foot another thorn is requisitioned, and when the thorn is taken out both are thrown away. So the bad tendencies are to be counteracted by the good ones, but after that, the good tendencies have also to be conquered.

Q: How can Vedanta be realized?

Swamiji: By 'hearing, reflection, and meditation'. Hearing must take place from a Sad-Guru [a real Guru]. Even if one is not a regular disciple, but is a fit aspirant and hears the Sad-Guru's words, he is liberated.

Q: Where should one meditate – inside the body or outside it? Should the mind be withdrawn inside or held outside?

Swamiji: We should try to meditate inside. As for the mind being here or there, it will take a long time before we reach the mental plane. Now our struggle is with the body. When one acquires a perfect steadiness in posture, then and then alone one begins to struggle with the mind. Asana [posture] being conquered, one's limbs remain motionless, and one can sit as long as one pleases.

Q: Sometimes one gets tired of Japa [repetition of the Mantra]. Should one continue it or read some good book instead?

Swamiji: One gets tired of Japa for two reasons. Sometimes one's brain is fatigued, sometimes it is the result of idleness. If the former, then one should give up Japa for the time being, for persistence in it at the time results in seeing hallucinations, or in lunacy, etc. But if the latter, the mind should be forced to continue Japa.

Q: Is it good to practise Japa for a long time, though the mind may be wandering?

Swamiji: Yes. As some people break a wild horse by always keeping his seat on his back.

Q: What is the efficacy of prayer?

Swamiji: By prayer one's subtle powers are easily roused, and if consciously done, all desires may be fulfilled by it, but done unconsciously, one perhaps in ten is fulfilled.

Q: You have written in your *Bhakti-Yoga* that if a weak-bodied man tries to practise Yoga, a tremendous reaction comes. Then what to do?

Swamiji: What fear if you die in the attempt to realize the Self! Man is not afraid of dying for the sake of learning and many other things, and why should you fear to die for religion? (V. 314-25)

EXPERIENCE AND VERIFICATION

Swamiji: One day in the temple-garden at Dakshineswar Sri Ramakrishna touched me over the heart, and first of all I began to see that the houses—rooms, doors, windows, verandahs—the trees, the sun, the moon—all were flying off, shattering to pieces as it were—reduced to atoms and molecules—and ultimately became merged in the Akasha [space]. Gradually again, the Akasha also vanished, and after that, my consciousness of the ego with it; what happened next I do not recollect. I was at first frightened. Coming back from that state, again I began to see the houses, doors, windows, verandahs, and other things. On another occasion, I had exactly the same realization by the side of a lake in America.

Disciple: Might not this state as well be brought about by derangement of the brain? And I do not understand what happiness there can be in realizing such a state.

Swamiji: A derangement of the brain! How can you call it so, when it comes neither as the result of delirium from any disease, nor of intoxication from drinking, nor as an illusion produced by various sorts of queer breathing exercises—but when it comes to a normal man in full posession of his health and wits? Then again, this experience is in perfect harmony with the Vedas. It also coincides with the words of realization of the inspired Rishis [sages] and Acharyas [teachers] of old. (V. 392)

HOW TO BE DETACHED

Almost all our suffering is caused by our not having the power of detachment. So along with the development of concentration we must develop the power of detachment. We must learn not only to attach the mind to one thing exclusively, but also to detach it at a moment's notice and place it upon something else. These two should be developed together to make it safe.

This is the systematic development of the mind. To me the very essence of education is concentration of the mind, not the collecting of facts. If I had to do my education over again, and had any voice in the matter, I would not study facts at all. I would develop the power of concentration and detachment, and then with a perfect instrument I could collect facts at will.

We should put our minds on things; they should not draw our minds to them. We are usually forced to concentrate. Our minds are forced to become fixed upon different things by an attraction in them which we cannot resist. To control the mind, to place it just where we want it, requires special training. (VI. 38-39)

HOW TO STUDY THE MIND

The mind uncontrolled and unguided will drag us down, down for ever—rend us, kill us; and the mind controlled and guided will save us, free us.

To study and analyse any material science, sufficient data are obtained. These facts are studied and analysed and a knowledge of the science is the result. But in the study and analysis of the mind, there are no data, no facts acquired from without, such as are equally at the command of all. The mind is analysed by itself. The greatest science, therefore, is the science of the mind, the science of psychology.

Deep, deep within, is the soul, the essential man, the Atman. Turn the mind inward and become united to that; and from that standpoint of stability, the gyrations of the mind can be watched and facts observed, which are to be found in all persons.

To control the mind you must go deep down into the subconscious mind, classify and arrange in order all the different impressions, thoughts, etc. stored up there, and control them. This is the first step. By the control of the subconscious mind you get control over the conscious. (VI. 30-32)

PRACTICAL HINTS ON MEDITATION

Swami Shuddhananda: What is the real nature of meditation?

Swamiji: Meditation is the focusing of the mind on some object. If the mind acquires concentration on one object, it can be so concentrated on any object whatsoever.

Disciple: Mention is made in the scriptures of two kinds of meditation – one having some object and the other objectless. What is meant by all that, and which of the two is the higher one?

Swamiji: First, the practice of meditation has to proceed with some one object before the mind. Once I used to concentrate my mind on some black point. Ultimately, during those days, I could not see the point any more, nor notice that the point was before me at all – the mind used to be no more – no wave of functioning would rise, as if it were all an ocean without any breath of air. In that state I used to experience glimpses of supersensuous truth. So I think the practice of meditation even with some trifling external object leads to mental concentration. But it is true that the mind very easily attains calmness when one practises meditation with anything on which one's mind is most apt to settle down. This is the reason why we have in this country [India] so much worship of the images of gods and goddesses. The real aim is to make the mind functionless, but this cannot be got at unless one becomes absorbed in some object.

Disciple: But if the mind becomes completely engrossed and identified with some object, how can it give us the consciousness of Brahman?

Swamiji: Yes, though the mind at first assumes the form of the object, yet later on the consciousness of that object vanishes. Then only the experience of pure 'isness' remains. (VI. 486-87)

SUPERNATURAL POWERS

Swamiji said, 'It is possible to acquire miraculous powers by some little degree of mental concentration,' and turning to the disciple he asked, 'Well, should you like to learn thought-reading? I can teach that to you in four or five days.'

Disciple: Of what avail will it be to me, sir?

Swamiji: Why, you will be able to know others' minds.

Disciple: Will that help my attainment of the knowledge of Brahman?

Swamiji: Not a bit.

Disciple: Then I have no need to learn that science.

Swamiji: Sri Ramakrishna used to disparage these supernatural powers; his teaching was that one cannot attain to the supreme truth if the mind is diverted to the manifestation of these powers. The human mind, however, is so weak that, not to speak of householders, even ninety per cent of the Sadhus [monks] happen to be votaries of these powers. In the West, men are lost in wonderment if they come across such miracles. It is only because Sri Ramakrishna has mercifully made us understand the evil of these powers as being hindrances to real spirituality that we are able to take them at their proper value. Haven't you noticed how for that reason the children of Sri Ramakrishna pay no heed to them? (VI. 515-17)

THE MYSTERY OF SAMADHI

Disciple: On the attainment of the absolute and transcendent Nirvikalpa Samadhi can none return to the world of duality through the consciousness of Egoism?

Swamiji: Sri Ramakrishna used to say that the Avataras [divine incarnations] alone can descend to the ordinary plane from that state of Samadhi, for the good of the world. Ordinary Jivas [individual souls] do not.

Disciple: When in Samadhi the mind is merged, and there remain no waves on the surface of consciousness, where then is the possibility of mental activity and returning to the world through the consciousness of Ego? When there is no mind, then who will descend from Samadhi to the relative plane, and by what means?

Swamiji: The conclusion of the Vedanta is that when there is absolute Samadhi and cessation of all modifications, there is no return from that state. But the Avataras cherish a few desires for the good of the world. By taking hold of that thread, they come down from the superconscious to the conscious state. (VII. 140)

THE POWER OF OJAS

The Yogis say that the part of the human energy which is expressed as sex energy, in sexual thought, when checked and controlled, easily becomes changed into Ojas.

Ojas is stored up in the brain, and the more

Ojas is in a man's head, the more powerful he is, the more intellectual, the more spiritually strong. One man may speak beautiful language and beautiful thoughts, but they do not impress people; another man speaks neither beautiful language nor beautiful thoughts, yet his words charm. Every movement of his is powerful. That is the power of Ojas.

It is only the chaste man or woman who can make the Ojas rise and store it in the brain; that is why chastity has always been considered the highest virtue. That is why in all the religious orders in the world which have produced spiritual giants, you will always find absolute chastity insisted upon. There must be perfect chastity in thought, word, and deed. (I. 169-70)

THE MASTERY OF LEARNING

A few days ago, a new set of the *Encyclopaedia Britanniaca* had been bought for the Belur Monastery. Seeing the new shining volumes, the disciple said to Swamiji, 'It is almost impossible to read all these books in a single lifetime.' He was unaware that Swamiji had already finished ten volumes and had begun the eleventh.

Swamiji: What do you say? Ask me anything you like from these ten volumes, and I will answer you all.

The disciple asked in wonder: 'Have you read all these books?'

Swamiji: Why should I ask you to question me otherwise?

Being examined, Swamiji not only reproduced the sense, but at places the very language of the difficult topics selected from each volume. The disciple, astonished, put aside the books, saying, 'This is not within human power!'

Swamiji: Do you see, simply by the observance of strict continence all learning can be mastered in a very short time – one has an unfailing memory of what one hears or knows but once. (VII. 223-24)

THE POWER OF THE MIND

The science of Raja-Yoga in the first place, proposes to give us such a means of observing the internal states. The instrument is the mind itself. The power of attention, when properly guided, and directed towards the internal world, will analyse the mind, and illumine facts for us. The powers of the mind are like rays of light dissipated; when they are concentrated, they illumine. This is our only means of knowledge.

The world is ready to give up its secrets if we only know how to knock, how to give it the necessary blow. The strength and force of the blow come through concentration. There is no limit to the power of the human mind. The more concentrated it is, the more power is brought to bear on one point; that is the secret. (I. 129-31)

MYSTERY-MONGERING

Anything that is secret and mysterious in these systems of Yoga [Raja-Yoga] should be at once rejected. The best guide in life is strength. In religion, as in all other matters, discard everything that weakens you, have nothing to do with it. Mystery-mongering weakens the human brain. It has well-nigh destroyed Yoga—one of the grandest of sciences. (I. 134)

FOLLOW THE MIDDLE PATH

A Yogi must avoid the two extremes of luxury and austerity. He must not fast, nor torture his flesh. He who does so, says the *Gita*, cannot be a Yogi: He who fasts, he who keeps awake, he who sleeps much, he who works too much, he who does not work, none of these can be a Yogi. (I. 136)

THE ROYAL PATH

The science of Raja-Yoga proposes to put before humanity a practical and scientifically worked out method of reaching this truth [immortality]. In the first place, every science must have its own method of investigation. If you want to become an astronomer and sit down and cry 'Astronomy! Astronomy!' it will never come to you. The same with chemistry. A certain method must be followed. You must go to a laboratory, take different substances, mix them up, compound them, experiment with them, and out of that will come a knowledge of chemistry. If you want to be an astronomer, you must go to an observatory, take a telescope, study the stars and planets, and then you will become an astronomer. Each science must have its own methods. I could preach you thousands of sermons, but they would not make you religious, until you practised the method. (I. 128)

EFFECTS OF MEDITATION

Day and night think and meditate on

Brahman, meditate with great one-pointedness of mind. And during the time of awakeness to outward life, either do some work for the sake of others or repeat in your mind, 'Let good happen to Jivas and the world!' 'Let the mind of all flow in the direction of Brahman!' Even by such continuous current of thought the world will be benefited. Nothing good in the world becomes fruitless, be it work or thought. Your thought-currents will perhaps rouse the religious feeling of some one in America. [Swamiji said this at the monastery of Belur Math, near Calcutta, speaking to an Indian disciple.] (VII. 237)

IN THE HOURS OF MEDITATION

You must keep the mind fixed on one object, like an unbroken stream of oil. The ordinary man's mind is scattered on different objects, and at the time of meditation, too, the mind is at first apt to wander. But let any desire whatever arise in the mind, you must sit calmly and watch what sort of ideas are coming. By continuing to watch in that way, the mind becomes calm, and there are no more thought-waves in it. Those things that you have previously thought deeply, have transformed themselves into a subconscious current, and therefore these come up in the mind in meditation.

The rise of these waves, or thoughts, during meditation is an evidence that your mind is tending towards concentration. Sometimes the mind is concentrated on a set of ideas —this is called meditation with Vikalpa or oscillation. But when the mind becomes almost free from all activities, it melts in the inner Self, which is the essence of infinite Knowledge, One, and Itself Its own support. This is what is called Nirvikalpa Samadhi, free from all activities. In Sri Ramakrishna we have again and again noticed both these forms of Samadhi. He had not to struggle to get these states. They came to him spontaneously, then and there. It was a wonderful phenomenon. It was by seeing him that we could rightly understand these things. (VII. 253-54)

EMOTIONS AND MEDITATION

Swamiji: Meditate every day alone. Every thing will open up of itself. During meditation suppress the emotional side altogether. That is a great source of danger. Those that are very emotional no doubt have their Kundalini rushing quickly upwards, but it is as quick to come down as to go up. And when it does come down, it leaves the devotee in a state of utter ruin. It is for this reason that Kirtanas [the singing of devotional songs] and other auxiliaries to emotional development have a great drawback. It is true that by dancing and jumping, etc. through a momentary impulse, that power is made to course upwards, but it is never enduring. On the contrary when it traces back its course, it rouses violent lust in the individual. But this happens simply owing to a lack of steady practice in meditation and concentration.

Disciple: Sir, in no scriptures have I ever read these secrets of spiritual practice. Today I have heard quite new things.

Swamiji: Do you think the scriptures contain all the secrets of spiritual practice? These are being handed down secretly through a succession of Gurus and disciples. Don't leave out a single day. If you have too much pressing work, go through the spiritual exercises for at least a quarter of an hour. Can you reach the goal without a steadfast devotion, my son? (VII. 254-55)

READ YOUR OWN LIFE

Control the mind, cut off the senses, then

you are a Yogi; after that, all the rest will come. Refuse to hear, to see, to smell, to taste; take away the mental power from the external organs. You continually do it unconsciously as when your mind is absorbed; so you can learn to do it consciously. The mind can put the senses where it pleases. Get rid of the fundamental superstition that we are obliged to act through the body. We are not. Go into your own room and get the Upanishads out of your own Self. You are the greatest book that ever was or ever will be, the infinite depository of all that is. Until the inner teacher opens, all outside teaching is in vain.

Books are useless to us until our own book opens; then all other books are good so far as they confirm our book. It is the strong that understand strength, it is the elephant that understands the lion, not the rat. How can we understand Jesus until we are his equals? Only grandeur appreciates grandeur, only God realizes God.

We are the living books, and books are but the words we have spoken. Everything is the living God, the living Christ; see it as such. Read man, he is the living poem. We are the light that illumines all the Bibles and Christs and Buddhas that ever were. Without that, these would be dead to us, not living. (VII. 71, 89)

EIGHT LIMBS OF YOGA

Raja-Yoga is known as the eightfold Yoga, because it is divided into eight principal parts. These are:

First: Yama. This is the most important and has to govern the whole life; it has five divisions:

Ist. Not injuring any being by thought, word, or deed.

2nd. Non-covetousness in thought, word, or deed.

3rd. Perfect chastity in thought, word, or deed.

4th. Perfect truthfulness in thought, word, or deed.

5th. Non-receiving of gifts.

Second: Niyama. The bodily care, bathing daily, dietary, etc.

Third: Asana, posture. Hips, shoulders, and head must be held straight, leaving the spine free.

Fourth: Pranayama, restraining the breath (in order to get control of the Prana or vital force).

Fifth: Pratyahara, turning the mind inward

and restraining it from going outward, revolving the matter in the mind in order to understand it.

Sixth: Dharana, concentration on one subject.

Seventh: Dhyana, meditation.

Eighth: Samadhi, illumination, the aim of all our efforts.

He who seeks to come to God through Raja-Yoga must be strong mentally, physically, morally, and spiritually. Take every step in that light. (VIII. 41, 44)

AT THE THRESHOLD

This is a lesson seeking to bring out the individuality. Each individuality must be cultivated. All will meet at the centre. 'Imagination is the door to inspiration and the basis of all thought.' All prophets, poets, and discoverers have had great imaginative power. The explanation of nature is in us; the stone falls outside, but gravitation is in us, not outside.

Those who stuff themselves, those who starve themselves, those who sleep too much, those who sleep too little, cannot become Yogis. Ignorance, fickleness, jealousy, laziness, and excessive attachment are the great enemies to success in Yoga practice. The three great requisites are:

First: Purity, physical and mental; all uncleanness, all that would draw the mind down, must be abandoned.

Second: Patience; at first there will be wonderful manifestations, but they will all cease. This is the hardest period, but hold fast; in the end the gain is sure if you have patience.

Third: Perseverance; persevere through thick and thin, through health and sickness, never miss a day in practice. (VIII. 38)

THE MIND AND ITS ASPECTS

The internal organ or mind has four aspects:

First: Manas, the cogitating or thinking faculty, which is usually almost entirely wasted, because uncontrolled; properly governed, it is a wonderful power.

Second: Buddhi, the will (sometimes called the intellect).

Third: Ahamkara, the self-conscious egotism (from Aham).

Fourth: Chitta, the substance in and through which all the faculties act, the floor of the mind as it were; or the sea in which the various faculties are waves.

Yoga is the science by which we stop Chitta from assuming, or becoming transformed into, several faculties. As the reflection of the moon on the sea is broken or blurred by the waves, so is the reflection of the Atman, the true Self, broken by the mental waves. Only when the sea is stilled to mirror-like calmness, can the reflection of the moon be seen, and only when the 'mind-stuff,' the Chitta is controlled to absolute calmness, is the Self to be recognized. (VIII. 39-40)

MEDITATE IN SILENCE

It is impossible to find God outside of ourselves. Our own souls contribute all the divinity that is outside of us. We are the greatest temple. The objectification is only a faint imitation of what we see within ourselves.

Concentration of the powers of the mind is our only instrument to help us see God. If you know one soul (your own), you know all souls, past, present, and to come. The concentrated mind is a lamp that shows us every corner of the soul.

Truth cannot be partial; it is for the good of all. Finally, in perfect rest and peace meditate upon It, concentrate your mind upon It, make yourself one with It. Then no speech is needed;

silence will carry the truth. Do not spend your energy in talking, but meditate in silence; and do not let the rush of the outside world disturb you. When your mind is in the highest state, you are unconscious of it. Accumulate power in silence, and become a dynamo of spirituality. (VII. 59-61)

MEDITATION ACCORDING TO VEDANTA

Swamiji's first night at Camp Taylor [Northern California], May 2, 1900. I close my eyes and see him standing there in the soft blackness with sparks from the blazing log fire flying through it and a day-old moon above. He was weary after a long lecture season, but relaxed and happy to be there. 'We end life in the forest,' he said, 'as we begin it, but with a world of experience between the two states.' Later after a short talk, when we were about to have the usual meditation, he said: 'You may meditate on whatever you like, but I shall meditate on the heart of a lion. That gives strength.' The bliss and power and peace of the meditation that followed could never be described.

(*Reminiscences of Swami Vivekananda:* Ida Ansell)

WHY GOD?

I have been asked many times, 'Why do you use that old word, God?' Because it is the best word for our purpose; you cannot find a better word than that, because all the hopes, aspirations, and happiness of humanity have been centred in that word. It is impossible now to change the word. Words like these were first coined by great saints who realized their import and understood their meaning. But as they become current in society, ignorant people take these words, and the result is that they lose their spirit and glory. The word God has been used from time immemorial, and the idea of this cosmic intelligence, and all that is great and holy, is associated with it. Do you mean to say that because some fool says it is not all right, we should throw it away? Another man may come and say, 'Take my word,' and another again, 'Take my word'. So there will be no end to foolish words. Use the old word, only use it in the true spirit, cleanse it of superstition, and realize fully what this great ancient word means. (II. 210)

THE VEDANTIC CONCEPTION OF GOD

What is the God of Vedanta? He is principle, not person. You and I are all Personal Gods. The absolute God of the universe, the creator, preserver, and destroyer of the universe, is impersonal principle. You and I, the cat, rat, devil and ghost, all these are Its persons – all are Personal Gods. You want to worship Personal Gods. It is the worship of your own self. If you take my advice, you will never enter any church. Come out and go and wash off. Wash yourself again and again until you are cleansed of all the superstitions that have clung to you through the ages.

I have been asked many times, 'Why do you laugh so much and make so many jokes?' I become serious sometimes – when I have stomach-ache! The Lord is all blissfulness. He is the reality behind all that exists, He is the goodness, the truth in everything. You are His incarnations. That is what is glorious. The nearer you are to Him, the less you will have occasions to cry or weep. The further we are from Him, the more will long faces come. The more we know of Him, the more misery vanishes.

God is the infinite, impersonal being – ever existent, unchanging, immortal, fearless; and you are all His incarnations, His embodiments. This is the God of Vedanta, and His heaven is everywhere. (VIII. 133-34)

THE GOAL AND METHODS OF REALIZATION

As every science has its methods, so has every religion. The methods of attaining the end of religion are called Yoga by us, and the different forms of Yoga that we teach, are adapted to the different natures and temperaments of men. We classify them in the following way, under four heads:

1. *Karma-Yoga:* The manner in which a man realizes his own divinity through works and duty.

2. *Bhakti-Yoga:* The realization of the divinity through devotion to, and love of, a Personal God.

3. *Raja-Yoga:* The realization of the divinity through the control of mind.

4. *Jnana-Yoga:* The realization of a man's own divinity through knowledge.

These are all different roads leading to the same centre – God. (V. 292)

PRAY FOR ILLUMINATION

Pray for illumination:

'I meditate on the glory of that Being who created this universe; may He illuminate my mind.'

Sit and meditate on this ten or fifteen minutes.

Tell your experience to no one but your Guru.

Talk as little as possible.

Keep your thoughts on virtue; what we think we tend to become.

Holy meditation helps to burn out all mental impurities. (VIII. 39)

DE-HYPNOTIZATION

Meditation has been laid stress upon by all religions. The meditative state of mind is declared by the Yogis to be the highest state in which the mind exists. When the mind is studying the external object, it gets identified with it, loses itself. To use the simile of the old Indian philosopher: the soul of man is like a piece of crystal, but it takes the colour of whatever is near it. Whatever the soul touches ... it has to take its colour. That is the difficulty. That constitutes the bondage. The colour is so strong, the crystal forgets itself and identifies itself with the colour. Suppose a red flower is near the crystal and the crystal takes the colour and forgets itself, thinks it is red. We have taken the colour of the body and have forgotten what we are. All our fears, all worries, anxieties, troubles, mistakes, weakness, evil, are from that one great blunder – that we are bodies.

The practice of meditation is pursued. The crystal knows what it is, takes its own colour. It is meditation that brings us nearer to truth than anything else. (IV. 227)

HERE AND NOW

Do not wait to have a harp and rest by degrees; why not take a harp and begin here? Why wait for heaven? Make it here.

How can we understand that Moses saw God unless we too see him? If God ever came to anyone, He will come to me. I will go to God direct, let Him talk to me. I cannot take belief as a basis; that is atheism and blasphemy. If God spoke to a man in the deserts of Arabia two thousand years ago, He can also speak to me today, else how can I know that He has not died? Come to God any way you can; only come. But in coming do not push anyone down. (VII. 93, 97)

AN INDIAN LULLABY

There was once a Hindu queen, who so much desired that all her children should attain freedom in this life that she herself took all the care of them; and as she rocked them to sleep, she sang always the one song to them – 'Tat tvam asi, Tat tvam asi' ('That thou art, that thou art').

Three of them became Sannyasins [monks], but the fourth was taken away to be brought up elsewhere to become a king. As he was leaving home, the mother gave him a piece of paper which he was to read when he grew to manhood. On that piece of paper was written, 'God alone is true. All else is false. The soul never kills or is killed. Live alone or in the company of holy ones.' When the young prince read this, he too at once renounced the world and became a Sannyasin. (VII. 89-90)

A TALE OF TWO BIRDS

The whole of the Vedanta philosophy is in this story :

Two birds of golden plumage sat on the same tree. The one above, serene, majestic, immersed in his own glory; the one below restless and eating the fruits of the tree, now sweet, now bitter. Once he ate an exceptionally bitter fruit, then he paused and looked up at the majestic bird above; but he soon forgot about the other bird and went on eating the fruits of the tree as before. Again he ate a bitter fruit, and this time he hopped up a few boughs nearer to the bird at the top. This happened many times until at last the lower bird came to the place of the upper bird and lost himself. He found all at once that there had never been two birds, but that he was all the time that upper bird, serene, majestic, and immersed in his own glory. (VII. 80)

BE GRATEFUL!

Be grateful to him who curses you, for he gives you a mirror to show what cursing is, also a chance to practise self-restraint; so bless him and be glad. Without exercise, power cannot come out; without the mirror, we cannot see ourselves.

The angels never do wicked deeds, so they never get punished and never get saved. Blows are what awaken us and help to break the dream. They show us the insufficiency of this world and make us long to escape, to have freedom. (VII. 69, 79)

FROM SOLITUDE TO SOCIETY

Swamiji: Shankara left this Advaita

[nondual] philosophy in the hills and forests, while I have come to bring it out of those places and scatter it broadcast before the workaday world and society. The lion-roar of Advaita must resound in every hearth and home, in meadows and groves, over hills and plains. Come all of you to my assistance and set yourselves to work.

Disciple: Sir, it appeals to me rather to realize that state through meditation than to manifest it in action.

Swamiji: That is but a state of stupefaction, as under liquor. What will be the use of merely remaining like that? Through the urge of Advaitic realization, you should sometimes dance wildly and sometimes remain lost to outward sense. Does one feel happy to taste of a good thing all by oneself? One should share it with others. Granted that you attain personal liberation by means of the realization of the Advaita, but what matters it to the world? You must liberate the whole universe before you leave this body. Then only you will be established in the eternal Truth. Has that bliss any match, my boy? (VII. 162-63)

WHO CAN KNOW THE KNOWER?

Disciple: If I am Brahman, why don't I always realize it?

Swamiji: In order to attain to that realization in the conscious plane, some instrumentality is required. The mind is that instrument in us. But it is a non-intelligent substance. It only appears to be intelligent through the light of the Atman behind. Therefore, it is certain that you won't be able to know the Atman, the Essence of Intelligence, through the mind. You have to go beyond the mind. The real fact is that there is a state beyond the conscious plane, where there is no duality of the knower, knowledge, and the instrument of knowledge, etc. When the mind is merged, that state is perceived. Language cannot express that state. (VII. 141-42)

WHAT IS BEYOND?

The process of evolution, higher and higher combinations, are not in the soul, it is already what it is. They are in nature. Suppose here is a screen, and behind the screen is wonderful scenery. There is one small hole in the screen through which we can catch only a little bit of that scenery behind. Suppose that hole becomes increased in size. As the hole increases in size, more and more of the scenery behind comes within the range of vision; and when the whole screen has disappeared, there is nothing between the scenery and you; you see the whole of it. This screen is the mind of man. Behind it is the majesty, the purity, the infinite power of the soul, and as the mind becomes clearer and clearer, purer and purer, more of the majesty of the soul manifests itself. Not that the soul is changing, but the change is in the screen. The soul is the unchangeable One, the immortal, the pure, the ever-blessed One. (VI. 24)

BE THE WITNESS!

Say, when the tyrant hand is on your neck, 'I am the Witness! I am the Witness!' Say, 'I am the Spirit! Nothing external can touch me.' When evil thoughts arise, repeat that, give that sledge-hammer blow on their heads, 'I am the Spirit! I am the Witness, the Ever-Blessed! I have no reason to do, no reason to suffer, I have finished with everything, I am the Witness. I am in my picture gallery – this universe is my museum. I am looking at these successive paintings. They are all beautiful, whether good or evil. I see the marvellous skill, but it is all one. Infinite flames of the Great Painter!' (V. 254)

DO WE WANT GOD?

Let us ask ourselves each day: 'Do we want

God?' When we begin to talk religion, and especially when we take a high position and begin to teach others, we must ask ourselves the same question. I find many times that I don't want God, I want bread more. I may go mad if I don't get a piece of bread; many ladies will go mad if they don't get a diamond pin, but they do not have the same desire for God; they do not know the only Reality that is in the universe. There is a proverb in our language: If I want to be a hunter, I'll hunt the rhinoceros; if I want to be a robber, I'll rob the king's treasury. What is the use of robbing beggars or hunting ants? So if you want to love, love God. (IV. 20)

THE SOUL AND ITS BONDAGE

We are the Infinite Being of the universe and have become materialized into these little beings, men and women, depending upon the sweet word of one man, or the angry word of another, and so forth. What a terrible dependence, what a terrible slavery! If you pinch my body, I feel pain. If one says a kind word, I begin to rejoice. See my condition—slave of the body, slave of the mind, slave of the world, slave of a good word, slave of a bad word, slave of passion, slave of happiness, slave of life, slave of death, slave of everything! This slavery has to be broken. How? Think always: 'I am Brahman.'

So what is the meditation of the Jnani [follower of the path of knowledge]? He wants to rise above every idea of body or mind, to drive away the idea that he is the body. Why make the body nice? To enjoy the illusion once more? To continue the slavery? Let it go, I am not the body. That is the way of the Jnani. The Bhakta says, 'The Lord has given me this body that I may safely cross the ocean of life, and I must cherish it until the journey is accomplished.' The Yogi says, 'I must be careful of the body, so that I may go on steadily and finally attain liberation.' (III. 25, 27-28)

IT IS ALL IN FUN

It is all play. Play! God almighty plays. That is all. You are the almighty God playing. If you want to play on the side and take the part of a beggar, you are not to blame someone else for making that choice. You enjoy being the beggar. You know your real nature to be divine. You are the king and play you are a beggar. It is all fun. Know it and play. That is all there is to it. Then practise it. The whole universe is a vast play. All is good because all is fun.

When I was a child I was told by someone that God watches everything. I went to bed and looked up and expected the ceiling of the room to open. Nothing happened. Nobody is watching us except ourselves. No Lord except our own Self.

Do not be miserable! Do not repent! What is done is done. If you burn yourself, take the consequences.

Be sensible. We make mistakes; what of that? That is all in fun. They go so crazy over their past sins, moaning and weeping and all that. Do not repent! After having done work, do not think of it. Go on! Stop not! Don't look back! What will you gain by looking back?

He who knows that he is free is free; he who knows that he is bound is bound. What is the end and aim of life? None, because I know that I am the infinite. If you are beggars, you can have aims. I have no aims, no want, no purpose. I come to your country, and lecture—just for fun. (II. 470-71)

A PSALM OF LIFE

In enjoyment is the fear of disease,
In high birth, the fear of losing caste,
In wealth, the fear of tyrants,
In honour, the fear of losing it,

In strength, the fear of enemies,
In beauty, the fear of old age,
In knowledge, the fear of defeat,
In virtue, the fear of scandal,
In the body, the fear of death.
In this life all is fraught with fear:
Renunciation alone is fearless.

(*In Search of God and Other Poems,* p. 81)

LET BYGONES BE BYGONES

If I teach you that your nature is evil, that you should go home and sit in sackcloth and ashes and weep your lives out because you took certain false steps, it will not help you, but will weaken you all the more, and I shall be showing you the road to more evil than good. If this room is full of darkness for thousands of years and you come in and begin to weep and wail, 'Oh the darkness,' will the darkness vanish? Strike a match and light comes in a moment. What good will it do you to think all your lives, 'Oh, I have done evil, I have made many mistakes?' It requires no ghost to tell us that. Bring in the light and the evil goes in a moment. Build up your character, and manifest your real nature, the Effulgent, the Resplendent, the Ever-Pure, and call It up in everyone that you see. (II. 357)

THE TAJ MAHAL OF TEMPLES

The living God is within you, and yet you are building churches and temples and believing all sorts of imaginary nonsense. The only God to worship is the human soul in the human body. Of course all animals are temples too, but man is the highest, the Taj Mahal of temples. If I cannot worship in that, no other temple will be of any advantage. The moment I have realized God sitting in the temple of every human body, the moment I stand in reverence before every human being and see God in him—that moment I am free from bondage, everything that binds vanishes, and I am free. (II. 321)

THE LORD IS YOURS

Do you feel for others? If you do, you are growing in oneness. If you do not feel for others, you may be the most intellectual giant ever born, but you will be nothing; you are but dry intellect, and you will remain so. And if you feel, even if you cannot read any book and do not know any language, you are in the right way. The Lord is yours.

Do you not know from the history of the world where the power of the prophets lay? Where was it? In the intellect? Did any of them write a fine book on philosophy, on the most intricate ratiocination of logic? Not one of them. They only spoke a few words. Feel like Christ and you will be a Christ; feel like Buddha and you will be a Buddha. It is feeling that is the life, the strength, the vitality, without which no amount of intellectual activity can reach God. It is through the heart that the Lord is seen, and not through the intellect. (II. 306, 307)

NO ONE TO BLAME

Blame none for your own faults, stand upon your own feet, and take the whole responsibility upon yourselves. Say, 'This misery that I am suffering is of my own doing, and that very thing proves that it will have to be undone by me alone.' That which I created, I can demolish; that which is created by some one else I shall never be able to destroy. Therefore, stand up, be bold, be strong. Take the whole responsibility on your own shoulders, and know that you are the creator of your own destiny. All the strength and succour you want is within yourselves. Therefore, make your own future. 'Let the dead past bury its dead.' The infinite future is before you, and you must always remember that each word, thought, and deed, lays up a store for you and that as the bad thoughts and bad works are ready to spring upon you like tigers, so also there is the inspiring hope that the good thoughts and good deeds are ready with the power of a hundred thousand angels to defend you always and for ever. (II. 225)

THE WORLD: NEITHER GOOD NOR BAD

If one millionth part of the men and women who live in this world simply sit down and for a few minutes say, 'You are all God, O ye men and O ye animals and living beings, you are all the manifestations of the one living Deity!' The whole world will be changed in half an hour. Instead of throwing tremendous bombshells of hatred into every corner, instead of projecting currents of jealousy and evil thought, in every country people will think that it is all He. He is all that you see and feel. How can you see evil until there is evil in you? How can you see the thief, unless he is there, sitting in the heart of your heart? How can you see the murderer until you are yourself the murderer? Be good, and evil will vanish for you. The whole universe will thus be changed.

Here is another thing to learn. We can not possibly conquer *all* the objective environments. We cannot. The little fish wants to fly from its enemies in the water. How does it do so? By evolving wings and becoming a bird. The fish did not change the water or the air; the change was in itself. Change is always subjective. All through evolution you find that the conquest of nature comes by change in the subject. Apply this to religion and morality, and you will find that the conquest of evil comes by the change in the subjective alone. That is how the Advaita system gets its whole force, on the subjective side of man. To talk of evil and misery is nonsense, because they do not exist outside.

I may make bold to say that the only religion which agrees with, and even goes a little further than modern researches, both on physical and moral lines is the Advaita, and that is why it appeals to modern scientists so much. (II. 287, 137-38)

AN ALLEGORY

Picture the Self to be the rider, and this body the chariot, the intellect to be the charioteer, mind the reins, and the senses the horses. He whose horses are well broken, and whose reins are strong and kept well in the hands of the charioteer (the intellect) reaches the goal which is the state of Him, the Omnipresent. But the man whose horses (the senses) are not controlled, nor the reins (the mind) well managed, goes to destruction. (II. 169)

MORALITY AND RELIGION

Religion comes when that actual realization in our own souls begins. That will be the dawn of religion; and then alone we shall be moral. Now we are not much more moral than the animals. We are only held down by the whips of society. If society said today, 'I will not punish you if you steal,' we should just make a rush for each other's property. It is the policeman that makes us moral. It is social opinion that makes us moral, and really we are little better than animals. We understand how much this is so in the secret of our own hearts. So let us not be hypocrites.

This is the watchword of the Vedanta—realize religion, no talking will do. But it is done with great difficulty. He has hidden Himself inside the atom, this Ancient One who resides in the inmost recess of every human heart. The sages realized Him through the power of introspection. (II. 164-65)

SEE GOD IN EVERYTHING

From my childhood I have heard of seeing

God everywhere and in everything, and then I can really enjoy the world, but as soon as I mix with the world, and get a few blows from it, the idea vanishes. I am walking in the street thinking that God is in every man, and a strong man comes along and gives me a push and I fall flat on the footpath. Then I rise up quickly with clenched fist, the blood has rushed to my head, and the reflection goes. Immediately I have become mad. Everything is forgotten; instead of encountering God I see the devil. Ever since we were born we have been told to see God in all. Every religion teaches that – see God in everything and everywhere.

Never mind failures; they are quite natural, they are the beauty of life, these failures. What would life be without them? It would not be worth having if it were not for struggles. Where would be the poetry of life? Never mind the struggles, the mistakes. I never heard a cow tell a lie but it is only cow – never a man. So never mind these failures, these little backslidings; hold the ideal a thousand times, and if you fail a thousand times, make the attempt once more. The ideal of man is to see God in everything. (II. 151-52)

TOWARDS THE GOAL SUPREME

If a man plunges headlong into foolish

luxuries of the world without knowing the truth, he has missed his footing, he cannot reach the goal. And if a man curses the world, goes into a forest, mortifies his flesh, and kills himself little by little by starvation, makes his heart a barren waste, kills out all feelings, and becomes harsh, stern, and dried up that man also has missed the way. These are the two extremes, the two mistakes at either end. Both have lost the way, both have missed the goal.

Unfortunately in this life, the vast majority of persons are groping through this dark life without any ideal at all. If a man with an ideal makes a thousand mistakes, I am sure that the man without an ideal makes fifty thousand. Therefore, it is better to have an ideal. And this ideal we must hear about as much as we can, till it enters into our hearts, into our brains, into our very veins, until it tingles in every drop of our blood and permeates every pore in our body. We must meditate upon it. 'Out of the fullness of the heart the mouth speaketh,' and out of the fullness of the heart the hand works too. (II. 150, 152)

WHAT MAKES US MISERABLE?

The cause of all miseries from which we suffer is desire. You desire something, and the desire is not fulfilled; and the result is distress.

If there is no desire, there is no suffering. But here, too, there is the danger of my being misunderstood. So it is necessary to explain what I mean by giving up desire and becoming free from all misery. The walls have no desire and they never suffer. True, but they never evolve. This chair has no desires, it never suffers; but it is always a chair. There is a glory in happiness, there is a glory in suffering.

As for me, I am glad I have done something good and many things bad; glad I have done something right, and glad I have committed many errors, because every one of them has been a great lesson. I, as I am now, am the resultant of all I have done, all I have thought. Every action and thought have had their effect, and these effects are the sum total of my progress.

The solution is this: Not that you should not have property, not that you should not have things which are necessary and things which are even luxuries. Have all that you want, and more, only know the truth and realize it. Wealth does not belong to anybody. Have no idea of proprietorship, possessorship. All belongs to the Lord. (II. 147-48)

QUINTESSENCE OF VEDANTA

Here I can only lay before you what the

Vedanta seeks to teach, and that is the deification of the world. The Vedanta does not in reality denounce the world. The ideal of renunciation nowhere attains such a height as in the teachings of the Vedanta. But, at the same time, dry suicidal advice is not intended; it really means deification of the world – giving up the world as we think of it, as we know it, as it appears to us – and to know what it really is. Deify it; it is God alone. We read at the commencement of one of the oldest of the Upanishads, 'Whatever exists in this universe is to be covered with the Lord.'

We have to cover everything with the Lord Himself, not by a false sort of optimism, not by blinding our eyes to the evil, but by really seeing God in everything. Thus we have to give up the world, and when the world is given up, what remains? God. What is meant? You can have your wife; it does not mean that you are to abandon her, but that you are to see God in the wife. Give up your children; what does that mean? To turn them out of doors, as some human brutes do in every country? Certainly not. That is diabolism; it is not religion. But see God in your children. So, in everything. In life and in death, in happiness and in misery, the Lord is equally present. The whole world is full of the Lord. Open your eyes and see

Him. This is what Vedanta teaches.

A tremendous assertion indeed! Yet that is the theme which the Vedanta wants to demonstrate, to teach, and to preach. (II. 146-47)

'WHY WEEPEST THOU, MY FRIEND?'

'Why weepest thou, my friend? There is neither birth nor death for thee. Why weepest thou? There is no disease nor misery for thee, but thou art like the infinite sky; clouds of various colours come over it, play for a moment, then vanish, But the sky is ever the same eternal blue.' Why do we see wickedness? There was a stump of a tree, and in the dark, a thief came that way and said, 'That is a policeman.' A young man waiting for his beloved saw it and thought that it was his sweetheart. A child who had been told ghost stories took it for a ghost and began to shriek. But all the time it was the stump of a tree. We see the world as we are.

Do not talk of the wickedness of the world and all its sins. Weep that you are bound to see wickedness yet. Weep that you are bound to see sin everywhere, and if you want to help the world, do not condemn it. Do not weaken it more. For what is sin and what is misery and what are all these, but the results of weakness?

The world is made weaker and weaker every day by such teachings. Men are taught from childhood that they are weak and sinners. Teach them that they are all glorious Children of immortality, even those who are the weakest in manifestation. Let positive, strong, helpful thought enter into their brains from very childhood. (II. 86-87)

THE SNARE OF MAYA

Once Narada [a great sage] said to Krishna, 'Lord, show me Maya [Cosmic Illusion].' A few days passed away, and Krishna asked Narada to make a trip with him towards a desert and after walking for several miles, Krishna said, 'Narada, I am thirsty; can you fetch some water for me?' 'I will go at once, sir, and get you water.' So Narada went.

At a little distance there was a village; he entered the village in search of water and knocked at a door, which was opened by a most beautiful young girl. At the sight of her he immediately forgot that his Master was waiting for water, perhaps dying for the want of it. He forgot everything and began to talk with the girl. All that day he did not return to his Master. The next day, he was again at the house, talking to the girl. The talk ripened into love; he asked the father for the daughter, and they were married and lived there and had children. Thus twelve years passed. His father-in-law died, he inherited his property. He lived, as he seemed to think, a very happy life with his wife and children, his fields and his cattle, and so forth.

Then came a flood. One night the river rose until it overflowed its banks and flooded the whole village. Houses fell, men and animals were swept away and drowned, and everything was floating in the rush of the stream. Narada had to escape. With one hand he held his wife, and with the other two of his children; another child was on his shoulders, and he was trying to ford this tremendous flood. After a few steps he found the current was too strong, and the child on his shoulders fell and was borne away. A cry of despair came from Narada. In trying to save that child, he lost his grasp upon one of the others, and it also was lost. At last his wife, whom he clasped with all his might, was torn away by the current, and he was thrown on the bank, weeping and wailing in bitter lamentation.

Behind him there came a gentle voice: 'My child, where is the water? You went to fetch a pitcher of water, and I am waiting for you. You have been gone for quite half an hour.' 'Half an hour!' Narada exclaimed. Twelve whole years had passed through his mind, and all these scenes had happened in half an hour!

And this is Maya. (II. 120-21)

LIFE INSPIRES LIFE

A man comes; you know he is very learned, his language is beautiful, and he speaks to you by the hour; but he does not make any impression. Another man comes, and he speaks a few words, not well arranged, ungrammatical perhaps; all the same, he makes an immense impression. Many of you have seen that. So it is evident that words alone cannot always produce an impression. Words, even thoughts contribute only one-third of the influence in making an impression, the man, two-thirds. What you call the personal magnetism of the man – that is what goes out and impresses you.

Coming to great leaders of mankind, we always find that it was the personality of the man that counted. Now, take all the great authors of the past, the great thinkers. Really speaking, how many thoughts have they thought? Take all the writings that have been left to us by the past leaders of mankind; take each one of their books and appraise them.

The real thoughts, new and genuine, that have been thought in this world up to this time amount to only a handful. Read in their books the thoughts they have left to us. The authors do not appear to be giants to us, and yet we know that they were great giants in their days. What made them so? Not simply the thoughts they thougnt, neither the books they wrote, nor the speeches they made, it was something else that is now gone, that is their personality. As I have already remarked, the personality of the man is two-thirds, and his intellect, his words, are but one-third. It is the real man, the personality of the man, that runs through us. (II. 14-15)

SPIRITUAL BOLDNESS

In the Mutiny of 1857 [the first freedom movement of India] there was a Swami, a very great soul, whom a Mohammedan mutineer stabbed severely. The Hindu mutineers caught and brought the man to the Swami, offering to kill him. But the Swami looked up calmly and said, 'My brother, thou art He, thou art He!' and expired.

Stand up, men and women, in this spirit, dare to believe in the Truth, dare to practise the Truth! The world requires a few hundred bold men and women. Practise that boldness which dares know the Truth, which dares show the Truth in life, which does not quake before death, nay welcomes death, makes a man know that he is the Spirit, that, in the whole universe, nothing can kill him. Then you will be free. Then you will know your real Soul. 'This Atman is first to be heard, then thought about and then meditated upon.' (II. 85)

A WISP OF STRAW

In some oil mills in India, bullocks are used that go round and round to grind the oil-seed. There is a yoke on the bullock's neck. They have a piece of wood protruding from the yoke, and on that is fastened a wisp of straw. The bullock is blindfolded in such a way that it can only look forward, and so it stretches its neck to get at the straw; and in doing so, it pushes the piece of wood out a little further; and it makes another attempt with the same result, and yet another, and so on. It never catches the straw, but goes round and round in the hope of getting it and in so doing, grinds out the oil. In the same way you and I who are born slaves to nature, money and wealth, wives and children, are always chasing a wisp of straw, a mere chimera, and are going through an innumerable round of lives without obtaining what we seek.

Such is the life-story of each one of us; such is the tremendous power of nature over us. It repeatedly kicks us away, but still we pursue it with feverish excitement. (I. 408-09)

LOVE ABIDETH FOREVER

Say day and night, 'Thou art my father, my mother, my husband, my love, my lord, my God – I want nothing but Thee, nothing but Thee, nothing but Thee.' Wealth goes, beauty vanishes, life flies, powers fly – but the Lord abideth for ever, love abideth for ever.

Stick to God! Who cares what comes to the body or to anything else! Through the terrors of evil, say – my God, my love! Through the pangs of death, say – my God, my love! Through all the evils under the sun, say – my God, my love!

This life is a great chance. What, seekest thou the pleasures of the world? – He is the fountain of all bliss. Seek for the highest, aim at that highest, and you *shall* reach the highest. (VI. 262)

MAN, THE MAKER OF HIS DESTINY

Weak men, when they lose everything and feel themselves weak, try all sorts of uncanny methods of making money, and come to astrology and all these things. 'It is the coward and the fool who says, "This is fate." ' But it is the strong man who stands up and says, 'I will make my fate.'

There is an old story of an astrologer who came to a king and said, 'You are going to die in six months.' The king was frightened out of his wits and was almost about to die then and there from fear. But his minister was a clever man, and this man told the king that these astrologers were fools. The king would not believe him. So the minister saw no other way to make the king see that they were fools but to invite the astrologer to the palace again. There he asked him if his calculations were correct. The astrologer said that there could not be a mistake, but to satisfy him he went through the whole of the calculations again and then said that they were perfectly correct. The king's face became livid. The minister said to the astrologer, 'And when do you think you will die?' 'In twelve years,' was the reply. The minister quickly drew his sword and separated the astrologer's head from the body and said to the king, 'Do you see this liar? He is dead this moment.' (VIII. 184-85)

THE GOSPEL OF FEARLESSNESS

What makes the difference between God

and man, between the saint and the sinner? Only ignorance. What is the difference between the highest man and the lowest worm that crawls under your feet? Ignorance. That makes all the difference. The infinite divinity is unmanifested, it will have to be manifested. This is spirituality, the science of the soul.

Strength is goodness, weakness is sin. If there is one word that you find coming out like a bomb from the Upanishads, bursting like a bomb-shell upon masses of ignorance, it is the word fearlessness. And the only religion that ought to be taught is the religion of fearlessness. It is fear that brings misery, fear that brings death, fear that breeds evil. And what causes fear? Ignorance of our own nature.

Despair not. For you are the same whatever you do, and you cannot change your nature. Nature itself cannot destroy nature. Your nature is pure. It may be hidden for millions of aeons, but at last it will conquer and come out. Therefore the Advaita brings hope to every one and not despair. Its teaching is not through fear; it teaches, not of devils who are always on the watch to snatch you if you miss your footing – it has nothing to do with devils – but says that you have taken your fate in your own hands. Your own Karma [action] has manufactured for you this body, and nobody did it for you. And all the responsibility of good and evil is on you. This is the great hope. What I have done, that I can undo. (III. 159-61)

THE NEED FOR A GURU

The soul can only receive impulses from another soul, and from nothing else. We may study books all our lives, we may become very intellectual, but in the end we find that we have not developed at all spiritually. It is not true that a high order of intellectual development always goes hand in hand with a proportionate development of the spiritual side in Man. In studying books we are sometimes deluded into thinking that thereby we are being spiritually helped; but if we analyse the effect of the study of books on ourselves, we shall find that at the utmost it is only our intellect that derives profit from such studies, and not our inner spirit. This inadequacy of books to quicken spiritual growth is the reason why, although almost every one of us can *speak* most wonderfully on spiritual matters, when it comes to action and the living of a truly spiritual life, we find ourselves so awfully deficient. To quicken the spirit, the impulse must come from another soul.

The person from whose soul such impulse comes is called the Guru—the teacher; and the person to whose soul the impulse is conveyed is called the Shishya—the student. (III. 45)

THE QUALIFICATIONS OF THE STUDENT

Three things are necessary to the student who wishes to succeed:

First: Give up all ideas of enjoyment in this world and the next, care only for God and Truth. We are here to know truth, not for enjoyment. Leave that to brutes who enjoy as we never can. Man is a thinking being and must struggle on until he conquers death, until he sees the light. He must not spend himself in vain talking that bears no fruit. Worship of society and popular opinion is idolatry. The soul has no sex, no country, no place, no time.

Second: Intense desire to know Truth and God. Be eager for them, long for them, as a drowning man longs for breath. Want only God, take nothing else, let not 'seeming' cheat you any longer. Turn from all and seek only God.

Third: The six trainings: First—Restraining the mind from going outward. Second—Restraining the senses. Third—Turning the mind inward. Fourth—Suffering everything without murmuring. Fifth—Fastening the mind to one idea. Take the subject before you and think it out; never leave it. Do not count time. Sixth—Think constantly of your real nature. Get rid of superstition. Do not hypnotize yourself into a belief in your own inferiority. Day and night tell yourself what you really are, until you realize, actually realize your oneness with God. (VIII. 37)

ARE WE FIT FOR PARADISE?

Some poor fishwives, overtaken by a violent storm, found refuge in the garden of a rich man. He received them kindly, fed them, and left them to rest in a summer-house, surrounded by exquisite flowers which filled all the air with their rich perfume. The women lay down in this sweet-smelling paradise, but could not sleep. They missed something out of their lives and could not be happy without it. At last one of the women arose and went to the place where they had left their fish baskets, brought them to the summer-house, and then once more happy in the familiar smell, they were all soon sound asleep. (VIII. 29)

WHAT WE THINK WE BECOME

Thought is all important, for 'what we think

we become'. There was once a Sannyasin, a holy man, who sat under a tree and taught the people. He drank milk, and ate only fruit, and made endless 'Pranayamas,' and felt himself to be very holy.

In the same village lived an evil woman. Every day the Sannyasin went and warned her that her wickedness would lead her to hell. The poor woman, unable to change her method of life which was her only means of livelihood, was still much moved by the terrible future depicted by the Sannyasin. She wept and prayed to the Lord, begging Him to forgive her because she could not help herself.

By and by both the holy man and the evil woman died. The angels came and bore her to heaven, while the demons claimed the soul of the Sannyasin. 'Why is this!' he exclaimed. 'Have I not lived a most holy life, and preached holiness to everybody? Why should I be taken to hell while this wicked woman is taken to heaven?' 'Because,' answered the demons, 'while she was forced to commit unholy acts, her mind was always fixed on the Lord and she sought deliverance, which has now come to her. But you, on the contrary, while you performed only holy acts, had your mind always fixed on the wickedness of others. You saw only sin, and thought only of sin, so now you have to go to that place where only sin is'. (VIII. 19-20)

ENJOY THE MANGOES

The whole world reads Bibles, Vedas, and Korans; but they are all only words, syntax, etymology, philology, the dry bones of religion. The teacher who deals too much in words and allows the mind to be carried away by the force of words loses the spirit. It is the knowledge of the *spirit* of the scriptures alone that constitutes the true religious teacher. The network of the words of the scriptures is like a huge forest in which the human mind often loses itself and finds no way out.

Ramakrishna used to tell a story of some men who went into a mango orchard and busied themselves in counting the leaves, the twigs, and the branches, examining their colour, comparing their size, and noting down everything most carefully, and then got up a learned discussion on each of these topics, which were undoubtedly highly interesting to them. But one of them, more sensible than the others, did not care for all these things, and instead thereof, began to eat the mango fruit. And was he not wise? So leave this counting of leaves and twigs and notetaking to others. This kind of work has its proper place, but not here in the spiritual domain. You never see a strong spiritual man among the 'leaf-counters'. (III. 49-50)

STICK TO ONE

Every sect of every religion presents only one ideal of its own to mankind, but the eternal Vedantic religion opens to mankind an infinite number of doors for ingress into the inner shrine of divinity, and places before humanity an almost inexhaustible array of ideals, there being in each of them a manifestation of the Eternal One.

Yet the growing plant must be hedged round to protect it until it has grown into a tree. The tender plant of spirituality will die if exposed too early to the action of a constant change of ideas and ideals. Many people, in the name of what may be called religious liberalism, may be seen feeding their idle curiosity with a continuous succession of different ideals. With them, hearing new things grows into a kind of disease, a sort of religious drink-mania. They want to hear new things just by way of getting a temporary nervous excitement, and when one such exciting influence has had its effect on them, they are ready for another. Religion is with these people a sort of intellectual opium-eating, and there it ends. Eka-Nishtha or devotion to one ideal is absolutely necessary for the beginner in the practice of religious devotion. (III. 63-64)

THE TRANSFORMATION OF ENERGY

Unchaste imagination is as bad as unchaste action. Controlled desire leads to the highest result. Transform the sexual energy into spiritual energy, but do not emasculate, because that is throwing away the power. The stronger this force, the more can be done with it. Only a powerful current of water can do hydraulic mining. (VII. 69)

HOW TO BE ILLUMINED?

The illumined souls, the great ones that come to the earth from time to time, have the power to reveal the Supernal Vision to us. They are free already; they do not care for their own salvation – they want to help others.

Upon these free souls depends the spiritual growth of mankind. They are like the first lamps from which other lamps are lighted. True, the light is in everyone, but in most men it is hidden. The great souls are shining lights from the beginning. Those who come in contact with them have as it were their own lamps lighted. By this the first lamp does not lose anything; yet it communicates its light to other lamps. A million lamps are lighted; but the first lamp goes on shining with undiminished light. The first lamp is the Guru, and the lamp that is lighted from it is the disciple. (VIII. 115 ,113)

THE SECRET OF RESTRAINT

All outgoing energy following a selfish motive is frittered away; it will not cause power to return to you; but if restrained, it will result in development of power. This self-control will tend to produce a mighty will, a character which makes a Christ or a Buddha. Foolish men do not know this secret; they nevertheless want to rule mankind.

The ideal man is he who, in the midst of the greatest silence and solitude, finds the intensest activity, and in the midst of the intensest activity, finds the silence and solitude of the desert. He has learnt the secret of restraint, he has controlled himself. (I. 33-34)

MIND: THE LIBRARY OF THE UNIVERSE

Knowledge is inherent in man. No knowledge comes from outside; it is all inside. What we say a man 'knows', should in strict psychological language, be what he 'discovers' or 'unveils'; what a man 'learns' is really what he 'discovers', by taking the cover off his own soul, which is a mine of infinite knowledge.

We say Newton discovered gravitation. Was it sitting anywhere in a corner waiting for him? It was in his own mind; the time came and he found it out. All knowledge that the world has ever received comes from the mind; the infinite library of the universe is in your own mind. (I. 28)

GRACE AND SELF-EFFORT

Disciple: Is there, sir, any law of grace?

Swamiji: Yes and no.

Disciple: How is that?

Swamiji: Those who are pure always in body, mind, and speech, who have strong devotion, who discriminate between the real and the unreal, who persevere in meditation and contemplation—upon them alone the grace of the Lord descends. Sri Ramakrishna used to say sometimes, 'Do rely on Him; be like the dry leaf at the mercy of the wind'; and again he would say, 'The wind of His grace is always blowing, what you need to do is to unfurl your sail.'

Disciple: But of what necessity is grace to him who can control himself in thought, word, and deed? For then he would be able to develop himself in the path of spirituality by means of his own exertions!

Swamiji: The Lord is very merciful to him whom He sees struggling heart and soul for Realization. But remain idle, without any struggle, and you will see that His grace will never come.

Disciple: Sri Girish Chandra Ghosh once said to me that there could be no condition in God's mercy; there could be no law for it! If there were, then it could no longer be termed mercy. The realm of grace or mercy must transcend all law.

Swamiji: But there must be some higher law at work in the sphere alluded to by G.C. of which we are ignorant. Those are words, indeed, for the last stage of development, which alone is beyond time, space, and causation. But, when we get there, who will be merciful, and to whom, where there is no law of causation? There the worshipper and the worshipped, the meditator and the object of meditation, the knower and the known, all become one – call that Grace or Brahman, if you will. It is all one uniform homogeneous entity! (VI. 481-82 and V. 398-400)

THE GOAL AND THE WAYS

Each soul is potentially divine.

The goal is to manifest this Divinity within by controlling nature, external and internal.

Do this either by work, or worship, or psychic control, or philosophy – by one, or more, or all of these – and be free.

This is the whole of religion. Doctrines, or dogmas, or rituals, or books, or temples, or forms, are but secondary details.

'Ye children of immortality, even those who live in the highest sphere, the way is found; there is a way out of all this darkness, and that is by perceiving Him who is beyond all darkness; there is no other way.' (I. 124, 128)

MAYA AND FREEDOM

Let us not be caught this time. So many times Maya has caught us, so many times have we exchanged our freedom for sugar dolls which melted when the water touched them.

Don't be deceived. Maya is a great cheat.

Get out. Do not let her catch you this time. Do not sell your priceless heritage for such delusions. Arise, awake, stop not till the goal is reached.

Hold your money merely as a custodian for what is God's. Have no attachment for it. Let name and fame and money go; they are a terrible bondage. Feel the wonderful atmosphere of freedom. You are free, free, free! Oh blessed am I! Freedom am I! I am the Infinite! In my soul I can find no beginning and no end. All is my Self. Say this unceasingly.

(*Reminiscences of Swami Vivekananda*, pp. 185, 180)

SLEEP NO MORE

My ideal indeed can be put into a few words and that is: to preach unto mankind their divinity, and how to make it manifest in every movement of life.

One idea that I see clear as daylight is that misery is caused by *ignorance* and nothing else. Who will give the world light? Sacrifice in the past has been the law, it will be, alas, for ages to come. The earth's bravest and best will have to sacrifice themselves for the good of many, for the welfare of all. Buddhas by the hundred are necessary with eternal love and pity.

Religions of the world have become lifeless mockeries. What the world wants is character. The world is in need of those whose life is one burning love, selfless. That love will make every word tell like thunderbolt.

Bold words and bolder deeds are what we want. Awake, awake, great ones! The world is burning with misery. Can you sleep? (VII. 498)

REFERENCES

The Complete Works of Swami Vivekananda
(*Mayavati Memorial Edition:* Advaita Ashrama)

The references to the *Complete Works* (in the editions shown below) are indicated at the end of each selection by the volume number in roman numerals and page number in arabic numerals.

Volume I .....Fourteenth Edition, September 1972
Volume II ....Twelfth Edition, June 1971
Volume III ....Tenth Edition, April 1970
Volume IV ....Tenth Edition, June 1972
Volume V ....Ninth Edition, August 1970
Volume VI ....Ninth Edition, September 1972
Volume VII ....Seventh Edition, October 1969
Volume VIII ....Fifth Edition, November 1971

In Search of God and Other Poems (Calcutta: Advaita Ashrama, First Reprint 1972)

Reminiscences of Swami Vivekananda by His Eastern and Western Admirers (Advaita Ashrama, Second Edition 1964)